THE ANTIRACIST ROADMAP TO EDUCATIONAL EQUITY

ASCD MEMBER BOOK

Many ASCD members received this book as a
member benefit upon its initial release.

Learn more at:
www.ascd.org/memberbooks

Avis Williams
Brenda Elliott

THE ANTIRACIST ROADMAP TO EDUCATIONAL EQUITY

A Systemwide Approach for All Stakeholders

 ascd

Arlington, Virginia USA

2800 Shirlington Road, Suite 1001 • Arlington, VA 22206 USA
Phone: 800-933-2723 or 703-578-9600 • Fax: 703-575-5400
Website: www.ascd.org • Email: member@ascd.org
Author guidelines: www.ascd.org/write

Richard Culatta, *Chief Executive Officer;* Anthony Rebora, *Chief Content Officer;* Genny Ostertag, *Managing Director, Book Acquisitions & Editing;* Stephanie Bize, *Acquisitions Editor;* Mary Beth Nielsen, *Director, Book Editing;* Katie Martin, *Senior Editor;* Thomas Lytle, *Creative Director;* Donald Ely, *Art Director;* Bailey Gregory/The Hatcher Group, *Graphic Designer;* Cynthia Stock, *Typesetter;* Kelly Marshall, *Production Manager;* Christopher Logan, *Senior Production Coordinator;* Shajuan Martin, *E-Publishing Specialist;* Kathryn Oliver, *Creative Project Manager*

PAPERBACK ISBN: 978-1-4166-3255-9   ASCD product #123023
PDF EBOOK ISBN: 978-1-4166-3256-6; see Books in Print for other formats.

Quantity discounts are available: email programteam@ascd.org or call 800-933-2723, ext. 5773, or 703-575-5773. For desk copies, go to www.ascd.org/deskcopy.

ASCD Member Book No. FY23-12 (Dec. 2023 P). ASCD Member Books mail to Premium (P), Select (S), and Institutional Plus (I+) members on this schedule: Jan, PSI+; Feb, P; Apr, PSI+; May, P; Jul, PSI+; Aug, P; Sep, PSI+; Nov, PSI+; Dec, P. For current details on membership, see www.ascd.org/membership.

Library of Congress Cataloging-in-Publication Data

Names: Williams, Avis, author. | Elliott, Brenda, author.
Title: The antiracist roadmap to educational equity : a systemwide approach for all stakeholders / Avis Williams and Brenda Elliott.
Description: Arlington, Virginia, USA : ASCD, [2023] | Includes bibliographical references and index.
Identifiers: LCCN 2023032955 (print) | LCCN 2023032956 (ebook) | ISBN 9781416632559 (paperback) | ISBN 9781416632566 (pdf ebook)
Subjects: LCSH: Educational equalization—United States—Case studies. | Racism in education--United States—Prevention. | Teachers—Training of--Social aspects—United States.
Classification: LCC LC213.2 .W58 2023 (print) | LCC LC213.2 (ebook) | DDC 379.2/60973—dc23/eng/20230824
LC record available at https://lccn.loc.gov/2023032955
LC ebook record available at https://lccn.loc.gov/2023032956

33 32 31 30 29 28 27 26 25 24   1 2 3 4 5 6 7 8 9 10 11 12

THE ANTIRACIST ROADMAP TO EDUCATIONAL EQUITY

A Systemwide Approach for All Stakeholders

Foreword *by Robert Jackson* vii

Preface xi

Introduction: The Journey to Educational Equity 1

1 The Antiracist Curriculum 13

2 The Antiracist Teacher 25

3 The Antiracist School Leader 38

4 The Antiracist Central Office Team 50

5 The Antiracist District Leader 66

6 The Antiracist Community 77

Conclusion: Leading Systemic Change 91

Appendix: Case Studies 99

References 106

Index 114

About the Authors 118

FOREWORD

School systems throughout the United States are failing Black and Brown students. Students who are Black, Indigenous, or people of color (BIPOC) continue to lead the nation in suspensions, expulsions, and dropouts (Chen, 2023). About 16 percent of Black students (3 to 21 years old) receive special education services, higher than the national average (National Center for Education Statistics [NCES], 2019b); they are also "more likely to be identified with intellectual disability or emotional disturbance than all students with disabilities and more likely to receive a disciplinary removal than all students with disabilities" (U.S. Department of Education, 2021). Students who are BIPOC have less access to high-level math and science courses, a lack of access to other core courses, and lower enrollment in Advanced Placement courses (U.S. Department of Education Office for Civil Rights, 2014a).

These students have all the skills and intelligence to perform in school at high levels, but all school districts don't treat them as such. These students do not always see themselves, or people who look like them, in the curriculum being taught at their schools. They don't feel a connection with the material they are being taught or the environment in which they are being educated. In order to change these statistics, their culture, experiences, and identities must be validated, valued, and leveraged to help them navigate the school system.

As a student, I was suspended from school several times but received no follow-up or behavioral intervention. I didn't know a lot about racism, discrimination, and cultural barriers, but I knew what I was enduring as a student was not beneficial. I earned good grades but still found myself suspended for minor offenses. The cultural gap was very wide.

In 5th grade, the kids in my inner-city neighborhood were bused to an all-White suburban school. All of us were placed in remedial classes; we had to test our way out. Many of my classmates were frustrated, gave up, and just stayed put, but I worked hard to test out of those classes. I had made good grades at my previous school, where expectations were high, and I didn't understand why very little seemed to be expected of me at my new school. Several of my classmates dropped out of school—mentally, in middle school, and physically, in high school. Even though I slipped through the cracks and graduated, the experience scarred me for life.

In America, this narrative hasn't changed much. These same dynamics persist in school systems throughout the United States. Students of color spend more time engaged in educational activities that are well below their grade level, which perpetuates the issues and keeps these students below grade level; White students have four times as many high-quality, grade-level-appropriate lessons, which helps them succeed (TNTP, 2018). Black and Brown children continue to be underserved, underrepresented, and marginalized.

Our children need a curriculum that reflects their culture and gives them hope for their future. How can these students succeed without the same access as their White peers? We must set high expectations for our children who are BIPOC—and, more important, we must expect them to meet and exceed the standards set before them.

The Antiracist Roadmap to Educational Equity provides a concise analysis of the challenges in eliminating education gaps, as well as strategies and steps that any stakeholder can take to better address the needs of these students. Culturally responsive pedagogy is a must. In this book, Avis Williams and Bren Elliott offer clear instructions and strategies to help educators not only present students with rigorous grade-level curriculum but also help students develop their identity as learners. Everyone involved in the education system—teachers, school administrators, central district office staff, district administrators, and community members—can benefit from relevant and easy-to-apply strategies to challenge practice, policies, systems, and structures that contribute to inequitable outcomes.

Addressing educational equity is everyone's responsibility. This book offers solutions to the challenges of developing a growth mindset. If you want to know how to transition students from a safe space to a brave space, or how to address childhood trauma and poverty, or how to better connect with students from backgrounds different from your own, or how to be an effective antiracist educator, this book is a resource you need.

Robert Jackson
Atlanta, Georgia, USA

PREFACE

*Educational equity means that each child receives
what is needed to reach their full potential.*

—National Equity Project

Edward, a 13-year-old 7th grader, is Black. He was retained in kindergarten due to immaturity and has been suspended at least twice every year since 3rd grade.

Over the years, his teachers described him as disrespectful, defiant, and a know-it-all; few wanted him in their class. Even in elementary school, Edward was said to be unruly. He was often seated alone and given remedial work with little support. Staff complained that it was hard to reach Edward's parents, and some assumed that they just didn't care about their son's education. What they didn't know was that Edward's mother was working long hours as a nurse and his father was working overseas. They also didn't know that Edward's main caretaker was his sickly grandmother, who had come to need more and more care from her grandson. By middle school, Edward was regularly getting detention for falling asleep in class and loudly proclaiming that he hated school.

In the second half of Edward's 7th grade year, there was a change. Edward's new English teacher noticed his love for writing—how he would get lost in writing and not even hear the bell ring. In his writing, she saw evidence that he knew a lot more than his reluctance to speak up in class would suggest. Eventually, this teacher was able to meet with Edward's mother and arrange for him to be tested. It turned out that Edward's IQ was remarkably high. For the first time, a teacher had looked beyond his behavior and seen his brilliance. For the first time, he began receiving interest, encouragement, support, and the challenge he had been craving.

Have you ever taught or tried to reach a student like Edward? How successful were you, and how do you know? What systemic structures could support Edward and other students who may otherwise be failed by the U.S. education system? How can teachers and school leaders meet the needs of students who are not successful, for whatever reason?

During our collective 50 years of experience as educators, the two of us have served as classroom teachers and principals and in district-level roles, where we led teams establishing and implementing policies and practices that improve outcomes for children who are BIPOC. We understand that getting to equity in education is a journey, and the fact that you are reading our words tells us that you do, too. Before we share our "antiracist roadmap" to help you navigate this journey in your classroom, school, district, and community, we want to share with you a little of what has brought us to where we are now.

Avis's Journey as an Equity Champion

Born in Salisbury, North Carolina, to Earnest and Freddie Mae Bearthes, I am a middle child with four living siblings. A brother and sister died of sudden infant death syndrome before I was born. Some of my earliest memories are of living in a house in Salisbury that we called "the barn," presumably because we did not have running water. At that time, I was the youngest of three. My sister Felisa is 15 months older than me, and our brother Gabriel is 18 months older than her. My brother Jason was born when I was 9, and my sister Trina a year and half later.

I was the self-proclaimed black sheep of the family; my father chastised me daily. He nicknamed me Chubby, as I was heavier than my older sister. (This led to years of being weight conscious.) He told me that I would never amount to anything. Although my report card reflected mostly As, it was never deemed good enough, and even as an adult I do not understand why my father was so mean. Unfortunately, it got much worse.

Trauma

In 1986, Felisa graduated from high school, joined the U.S. Army, and left home. (Gabriel had done the same two years earlier.) When I started my senior year, my mother told me that once I graduated, she would leave my father. He was unemployed following a car accident, although he was physically capable of working. His interactions with my mother were becoming increasingly volatile. As I too prepared to join the army, I felt a sense of relief that my mother planned on leaving him and that my younger siblings would not endure the kind of childhood that I had experienced.

In September 1987, on the morning of my graduation from basic training, I was looking forward to seeing my family. After the ceremony, I was summoned to the chaplain's office, where I saw my older brother and sister but not my parents. My confusion was met with the horrifying news that on the day before, and in the presence of my younger siblings, my father had stabbed my mother 26 times, ending her life. My mother's death affected each of us differently. It was by far the most traumatic incident in my life, and I have come to see that both my battle with my weight and my being an overachiever were ways of proving my father wrong and making my mother proud.

Becoming Dr. Avis

After getting out of the army in 1991, my now-ex-husband and I started a personal training center in Huntsville, Alabama, competing in fitness competitions from 1992 to 1998. I enrolled in community college; our daughter, Bree, was born in 1994, and I graduated in 1995 with a bachelor's degree and a certification to teach English and physical education. My first teaching job was at a high-poverty high school, where I taught English in the morning and PE in the afternoon.

Although I was not familiar with the concept of "equity in education," it was clear to me that there was a problem. Many of my high school English students struggled with reading and lacked the background knowledge to successfully engage in our classroom discussions. Further, nearly half were either receiving special education services or had qualified for services based on their poor achievement. I volunteered to serve in various capacities: I coached the dance team and track, and I taught an Advanced Placement English class (with no AP training).

I went on to serve as a middle school English teacher and an assistant principal in a neighboring, more affluent school district. It was my first experience with the racial achievement gap: 70 percent of the students in this district were White and most were upper middle class. The majority of the Black students were poor and low performing. I started asking questions. Why were the Black students so far behind the White students? As the assistant principal, I questioned why so many Black males—despite comprising only about 11 percent of the student body—were being sent to my office for disciplinary reasons.

Data that our school collected to meet the reporting requirements of the No Child Left Behind Act further highlighted the fact that we were sorely failing our Black and Brown children. Despite the law, these young people, who looked like me, were indeed being left behind. I was motivated to intervene. I moved from questioning to reading and conducting research as I prepared to assume my first principal role in 2005.

From 2005 to 2009, I served as an elementary principal in a school in the highest-poverty community in Huntsville, where almost 97 percent of the students were Black. This experience shaped my beliefs as a leader and continues to drive my passion to seek equity in education for children who are BIPOC. In my earliest engagement with the complexity of equity work, I collaborated with a professor from Kentucky who was leading work in cultural competency and equity in education and served on teams conducting equity audits of school districts from several states.

With a greater understanding of the importance of school culture, I was more than prepared for my next job challenge. In spring 2009, when my school closed and consolidated with another, I had the opportunity to open a new technology middle school. With a mixed-income student body including military families, it was an ideal setting to explore technology integration, bullying prevention, and school culture. I (once again) replaced a male principal who had served the K–8 school for 20 years. In 2012, though, I felt my heart calling me home to North Carolina.

In a leap of faith, I took a pay cut and moved home to serve as a high school principal. The theme of replacing a veteran male principal continued, and, as a bonus, I was also the school's first Black principal. Despite my depth of knowledge about culturally responsive teaching, gang prevention and intervention, and closing achievement gaps, I was clearly *not* hired to take action on these measures. Pushback was immediate, and the racism shocked me. The school was purposely segregated by race, with limited opportunities for rigorous academic engagement for the Black students. Although just over half of the students were Black, enrollment in advanced classes was 90 percent White. The practice was so deeply rooted in the culture of the school and the community that even the Black families seemed to expect it.

This experience was an awakening for me that equity work, to be successful, had to be a district focus—or, even better, a community desire.

By fall 2013, I had found a better match in a much larger school district. There I led secondary curriculum and instruction for nearly 60 middle and high schools. One clear goal in this district included decreasing the achievement gap for African American boys. Our data showed that even when poverty was not a factor, these students performed significantly lower than their White counterparts. I gained new skills and built relationships that would support my future leadership endeavors. A highlight of this role was meeting Bren Elliott, who was the executive director of student services. Our departments did not work together, but we realized quickly the effects our combined efforts could have on improving student outcomes, especially for students who were BIPOC.

Selma Selma

In February 2015, I made the difficult decision to move back to Alabama, applying for a superintendent position in Selma. The magnitude of this opportunity was much on my mind when I attended the 50th Bridge Crossing Jubilee event commemorating Bloody Sunday. Oprah, Common, and President Obama participated, along with actors from the movie *Selma* and elected officials from across the nation.

I recall sharing my excitement with a friend and fellow educator, telling her that I was a finalist to be the superintendent of Selma City Schools. Her response was *"Selma* Selma?" From that point, we giddily referred to "Selma Selma" when speaking about the "Queen City of the Blackbelt." On the day of my interview, I traveled to Selma, toured schools, met district staff and board members, and interviewed in front of an audience at Selma High School. Days later, I learned that the job was offered to someone else. Disappointed, I continued to pursue two other superintendent positions and eventually accepted the role of assistant superintendent of curriculum in Tuscaloosa, Alabama. At the time, my daughter was a sophomore at the University of Alabama, and I could see Bryant Denny Stadium from my office. Roll Tide!

This position was a game changer for me: I reported directly to the superintendent and led a team of over 20. With a massive achievement gap due to the wealth gap in Tuscaloosa, there was a clear need for culturally responsive pedagogy and professional learning related to implicit bias and cultural competency. Over the two years I was there, we made progress through the collective efforts of our highly proficient team.

When the Selma superintendent position opened again in 2017, I applied and interviewed again—and this time was offered the position. I have always thrived in an environment where I faced great needs and where my leadership could make a difference. Selma was riddled with gang violence, crime, and high (and in some cases extreme) poverty—and faced a shrinking population. The district was under state intervention. The role presented many challenges, but I was ready to dive in. I *knew* that this was my dream job and an opportunity to make a difference to a beautiful community with so much potential. I was ready to lead the schools of "Selma Selma"—and did so successfully for five years.

We started the journey with a new strategic plan that included an updated mission, vision, and core values. Equity was added as a core value, and our team was intentional about removing barriers to success and providing access to rigorous instruction. We were released from state intervention, and, over the span of my tenure, we improved reading and math scores and graduation rates, added robotics teams to all schools, implemented restorative practices, created academies of academic excellence, and were awarded the Tier II

Performance Excellence Award based on the Baldrige Framework for Performance Excellence.

In 2022, I took on a new challenge as the first female superintendent of NOLA Public Schools in New Orleans. Ninety percent of our students are BIPOC. The journey continues.

I am immensely grateful to everyone who has contributed to the making of this book. My heartfelt appreciation goes out to the dedicated educators, passionate scholars, tireless researchers, and insightful practitioners who have paved the way for a more equitable educational landscape. I thank my former professor and friend, the late Dr. Harold Bishop of the University of Alabama, for modeling for me what it means to champion equity. To my daughter Bree, thank you for being such an inspiration and for reaffirming my "why." I extend my deepest thanks to my family, friends, and colleagues for their unwavering support, encouragement, and belief in me. Finally, to my co-author, Soror, sister, and friend, Dr. Bren Elliott, this book stands as a testament to our collective endeavor to create a more just and equitable world through education. I'm so glad we took this journey together.

Bren's Journey to Antiracist Education

The lineage of my family is diverse and complicated. It is very difficult to trace the lineages of African Americans due to chattel slavery in the United States. What I do know is that my paternal grandfather, Samuel Walter, was one of 10 children born to Charles Elliott and Alice King. The union of two enslaved Africans, Balum and Mary, yielded a beautiful brown baby named Charles, who was my Grandpa Sam's dad. Grandpa Sam's mother, Alice, was biracial—conceived when her mother, Ester, was raped by her enslaver, John King.

I can trace the lineage of my paternal grandmother, Mary Eliza Carver, back about 200 years. Grandma Mary's lineage is also very diverse but very different. In 1875, Cathran Howell, a White woman, gave birth to a child fathered by a Black man named Hardy Harris. Their son, John Harris, was my grandmother's father. Both Cathran Howell, my great-great-grandmother, and her mother, Penny Taylor, were prohibited from being buried in the cemetery for White people in Cumberland County, North Carolina, due to their relationships with Black people. These relatives are buried in our family grave plot, which can be found on the Fort Bragg reservation not far from our family home in Fayetteville, North Carolina. John Harris, my biracial great-grandfather, married Ann Carver, a Native American/Indigenous woman, and from that union, seven children were born—one of whom was my grandmother, Mary Eliza.

I have relatives who are Black, White, Native American, biracial, and multiracial. I am the result of the intermingling of European, African, and Indigenous American people. Sometimes I imagine what it must have been like for Balum and Mary, who were enslaved and working in the cotton fields of North Carolina, to be in love and bring forth children who in turn would be considered another person's property. Or for Cathran and Hardy to be in a biracial relationship in the South only 10 years after the end of slavery—a relationship that put their very lives at risk. Or what life was like for my Indigenous family members, John and Ann Carver, who escaped the Trail of Tears and the forced removal of more than 17,000 Native Americans from North Carolina. When I think of all of this and how their love was more powerful than all the forces that surrounded them, I am in awe of them and the fact that I am here today.

I was raised in North Carolina on the same lands that my great-grandparents lived on and eventually came to own. Although we were poor, I learned to read early, and my parents believed in education as a key to a great future. I grew up near Fort Bragg, a large military base. The schools I attended were relatively well funded and racially diverse. I was frequently taught by educators of color. I graduated in the top 10 percent of my class and went on to attend college on a full military scholarship. I left college believing that public education was the great equalizer, a way out of poverty.

It was only in 1994, when I became a public school teacher in a large inner-city high school, that I began to see the ways in which institutional, structural racism was narrowing children of color's opportunities to receive a great education. I began to see that my personal experiences in public education were not the experiences that most children of color had or were having. I began to see how teacher dispositions affected what children thought was expected of them and, thus, what was possible for them to achieve.

As a high school teacher and principal, I found myself working to convince some fellow educators, students, and their families that children of color were capable of learning at high levels. I am thankful for the many educators who shared my belief that all children, of all races and ethnicities, were capable of excelling in school—and who also believed that it was our responsibility to create the conditions that allowed them to do so. One of my greatest joys was leading the turnaround of an inner-city high school that had been persistently low performing. This work required mindset shifts, as well as building new instructional strategies and data interrogation skills. I noticed that many students had lost hope after years of participating in schooling that did not value them or provide them with clear connections to an exciting future. I added many field trips and college visits; students cannot dream about opportunities they don't know about. We also offered training to help families navigate the college application process, a destination that many had long thought unreachable.

I pushed my students to lean into the productive struggle that they were experiencing in their studies, as this was preparation for college. The most essential strategy for improving student performance outcomes was increasing access to rigorous, engaging grade-level curriculum. This is the thing: It is not enough for teachers to *care* about students. They must teach on grade level and assess on grade level. When teaching, assessment, and articulated curriculum are not aligned, assessment data is mostly a reflection of the socioeconomics of the school community. When we don't teach what is on the test, we can only measure what students bring to the table. And for children in low-wealth communities without access to a rigorous on-grade-level curriculum, that means measuring the gaps between their lived experiences and the middle-class, Eurocentric curriculum on which standardized tests are based.

To the Central Office

The teacher is the unit of change for a school, and the principal is the unit of change for the district. After I left my second principalship, I worked in several central office positions that gave me the opportunity to see more clearly the systemic opportunity gaps that lead to racial gaps in achievement and other student outcomes. As a principal supervisor, I coached principals to transform their schools through thoughtful strategic action focused on improving student engagement and the quality of instruction. In my next central office job, I oversaw the turnaround efforts of 24 high-priority schools—schools that had failed to make adequate yearly progress for four or more consecutive years. I provided coaching and support to school leaders; served as the district's liaison among central office staff, school staff, and state consultants; and authored plans for using federal funds to transform teaching and learning. One common denominator for all these schools was their students of color, whose gaps started early and failed to close. But we also had dedicated principals and teachers who simply lacked the resources to overcome significant gaps. I could replace ineffective staff; what took more time (but was just as important) was building teachers' and leaders' skills and capacity.

Going Home

In 2010, upon my youngest son's graduation from high school, I left Nashville and headed home to North Carolina. By 2012, I was working in student support services for a school district that was really digging deep into equity work; they even had a district-level equity director. I attended numerous trainings that provided space for district staff to interrogate race and racism in America and its structural underpinning of almost every system in America, particularly education.

When the district launched an initiative to address gaps for African American male students in both academic outcomes and disciplinary suspensions, I co-chaired the project focused on addressing the disparity in suspensions between these students and their peers. Our student discipline data revealed that Black male students were suspended from school at more than five times the rates of their White peers. Digging deeper into the data, we were able to determine that although the rate at which a discipline referral for a student ended up in a suspension was the same regardless of race, Black males were getting referred at a rate five times their White peers.

To really address this challenge, we needed to intercede at both the principal and teacher levels. We needed to address teacher mindsets (how they viewed Black children), their understanding of age-appropriate behavior, and the skills they had to build safe and nurturing classrooms. We needed to build our principals' capacity to analyze their data to get to the root causes of disparities, to be proficient in the skills needed to develop and to courageously implement strategies to address racialized trends. After one year of this initiative, we experienced a more than 50 percent reduction in suspension days for Black male students in the district.

Meeting Avis

It was during this work that I met Dr. Avis Williams, who was co-leading the initiative focused on racial disparities in literacy outcomes. As soon as we met, we realized that we had much more in common: We were both born in North Carolina, grew up in poverty, were U.S. Army veterans, and had been high school principals. Our common experiences had resulted in the two of us developing the same point of view regarding what was required to address long-seated racialized student outcomes in American public schools. It was inspiring to have someone with the same lens and passion for the work.

In 2017, I was recruited to come to Washington, DC, to serve as DC Public Schools' first chief equity officer. In this role, I would oversee key strategic equity levers such as leadership development, student services, and the school-based staff evaluation system. My experiences as a teacher, principal, and central office leader in urban schools and school districts gave me both the "in the trenches" and systemic experiences and perspectives to lead comprehensive equity work. And my military experience grounded me with the strategic planning expertise necessary to win this war.

I have had the honor of serving as a high school teacher, a middle and high school principal, a principal supervisor, and an assistant superintendent. Through these many experiences, I worked to create more equitable opportunities for students who were historically marginalized. I have had many successes and many failures. As a high school principal, I would tell my students, "Your choices impact your destiny; your destiny is in your hands"—and many former students have commented on social media about the effect of that statement on their lives. But destiny is much more complicated than a student's choice. Institutional racism, oppressive systems, and bias make it harder for students of color to thrive in schools. Although the students do have to commit to working hard, school and district staff, families, and the community can do a lot to make equitable outcomes more likely.

I am a woman of color four generations removed from legalized chattel slavery, one generation removed from state-sanctioned Jim Crow, and part of a generation affected by the new Jim Crow's legalized mass incarceration of people of color who is now working in our nation's capital, on the ancestral lands of the Anacostan and Nacotchtank peoples. I am still on my own personal antiracist journey. We live in a country that does an insufficient job of providing equitable education for most students of color, and yet I am still hopeful. Hopeful that through strategic and courageous action in public education, we can fulfill our Constitution's commitment to liberty and justice for all.

I extend my sincere gratitude to my ancestors, my former teachers and students, my educational colleagues, and everyone who has poured life into my life and into this project. I thank my two amazing sons, Brandon and Darrius, who were still in preschool when I first became a teacher almost 30 years ago for sharing me with so many other children and allowing me to see the world through the eyes of young men of color. To the "AWesome" Dr. Avis Williams, it has been an honor to co-create this roadmap with you and to imagine a world where all students experience a strong sense of belonging and succeed academically in school. Miles to go before we sleep. . . .

Our Journey Together

This book is for every educator and supporter of education who is interested in, curious about, or committed to creating antiracist schools where BIPOC children—children like Edward—are seen, heard, and empowered to bring their whole selves into the classroom every day.

Whether you are already a champion for equity or new to this work, this book will enhance your journey. There are millions of students who need teachers and leaders who believe in their potential and are willing to grow and learn what it means to support systemic change that creates more equitable and antiracist schools and districts.

INTRODUCTION: THE JOURNEY TO EDUCATIONAL EQUITY

Until we get equality in education,
we won't have an equal society.

—Sonia Sotomayor

Educational equity is the assurance that "every student has access to the educational resources and rigor they need at the right moment in their education across race, gender, ethnicity, language, disability, sexual orientation, family background, and/or family income" (America's Promise Alliance, Aspen Education & Society Program, & CCSSO, 2018, p. 5). The current model for education in the United States, however, is not effective in obtaining equitable education outcomes for all children. Racial gaps exist in almost every school-related outcome measure from kindergarten readiness to dropout rates, grade-point averages, college admission test scores, attendance and graduation rates, grade retention, out-of-school suspensions, honors and Advanced Placement course enrollment and passing rates, identification for gifted education versus identification for special education, and college enrollment and persistence (De Brey et al., 2019). In every single measure, marginalized students—specifically those who are Black, Indigenous, and people of color (BIPOC)—have significantly less positive outcomes than their White peers. These outcome gaps are often the largest and most persistent between Black students and White students (Shores et al., 2020).

Systemic Racism in Education

The terms *structural racism, institutional racism,* and *systemic racism* are often used interchangeably; they all refer to a system of structures with procedures or processes that disadvantage a particular group of people based on their race (see Glover & Miguel, 2020). One example of systemic racism is "redlining." Outlawed in 1968, redlining was used by banks and the real estate industry to identify neighborhoods where people of color lived; the name comes from literally outlining these areas on maps, using red ink. In these areas, the property value was less than in White neighborhoods, and it was harder to get loans to purchase homes there (Burke & Schwalbach, 2021).

Although the unanimous 1954 Supreme Court decision in *Brown v. Board of Education* declared school segregation unconstitutional, many public schools across this country remain segregated by socioeconomic status and race (Carrillo & Salhotra, 2022). Nationwide, hundreds of White, wealthy communities have seceded or attempted to secede from larger school districts (Sparks, 2019), leaving schools racially segregated and decreasing much-needed tax dollars allocated to predominantly Black schools. Although redlining is no longer legal, property in communities of color continues to be disproportionately undervalued (Perry et al., 2018). Because more than 35 percent of public school funds comes from property taxes, wealthier communities often end up with better-resourced schools. Predominantly non-White school districts in the United States annually receive $23 billion less than their majority-White counterparts (edbuild.org, n.d.). In addition to inequitable funding and de facto segregation, systemic racism in education includes lower expectations for students who are BIPOC, harsher disciplinary penalties for classroom infractions, and less access to rigorous curriculum (Alvarez, 2021).

Student discipline policies that disproportionately affect students who are BIPOC and the addition of security guards and school resource officers in schools can lead students to feel more policed than protected. The U.S. Department of Education Office for Civil Rights (2014b) has noted that Black, Hispanic male, and American Indian students are disciplined at school at a higher rate than their White counterparts. This includes school suspensions, expulsions, physical restraints, and arrests. The American Civil Liberties Union (2023) has also noted that 1.7 million students attend schools with security or police officers yet no guidance counselor or social worker.

The incarceration rate in the United States has grown by 500 percent over the past 40 years (Sentencing Project, 2023; see also Ghandnoosh & Nellis, 2022)—and schools are contributing to this increase. The National Education Association (2021–2022) has defined the *school-to-prison pipeline* as "policies and practices that are directly and indirectly pushing students of color out of school and on a pathway to prison, including . . . harsh school discipline policies that overuse suspension and expulsion" (p. 23). Increased policing and draconian disciplinary procedures are creating schools that look more like institutions for confining prisoners. When young people are going to court rather than to class, the school-to-prison pipeline is clearly in place.

The year 2020 saw uprisings against police brutality, sparked by the killings of Ahmaud Arbery, Breonna Taylor, George Floyd, and Rayshard Brooks. Beyond hashtags, Americans began to demand an overhaul of the criminal justice system and, concurrently, to address racial and social justice in other systems, such as housing, health care, and employment. Position statements from Fortune 500 companies like Netflix, Citigroup, and Microsoft voiced support for Black lives and opposition to racism (McGirt, 2020). In education, school and district leaders were similarly inspired to examine and address inequities that adversely affect students who are BIPOC.

Inequities in education have significant long-term fiscal effects. In 2013, the *For Each and Every Child* report of the Equity and Excellence Commission suggested that

> if Hispanic and African American student performance grew to be comparable to White performance and remained there over the next 80 years, [the] impact would be staggering—adding some $50 trillion (in present value terms) to our economy. This amount constitutes more than three times the size of our current GDP and represents the income that we forgo by not ensuring equity for all of our students. (p. 13)

Systemic racism in education has direct, detrimental effects on many students who are BIPOC and their families. The concomitant disadvantages affect overall quality of life, limiting access to postsecondary education and employment, income, and generational wealth.

Everyone with an interest in education—from teachers to administrators, students and their families, school board members, and those in surrounding communities—has a moral responsibility to examine the systems, structures, actions, policies, and practices that contribute to achievement gaps. We also have a moral responsibility to work to eliminate them.

A History of Racial Achievement Gaps in the United States

Racial achievement gaps are disparities in average academic achievement as measured by standardized test scores when comparing the achievement of students across racial lines. And these gaps are pervasive, persistent, and severe in school districts across our country.

Academic achievement data was first collected and disaggregated by race in America's public schools in 1940 by the U.S. Census Bureau. The metrics by which academic achievement is measured have changed quite extensively over the years, as has the population of students that has access to education. The majority of the more than 50 million students enrolled in U.S. public schools are children and youth of color (NCES, 2020), and the United States continues to become more racially and ethnically diverse (U.S. Census Bureau, 2021). What has *not* changed is the relationship between the achievement of White and Black students. Black students still persistently underperform on achievement measures when compared to their White peers.

Hanushek and colleagues (2019) examined the Black–White student achievement gap and the socioeconomic achievement gap from 1954 to the present. The results of their study, based on data from the National Assessment of Educational Progress (NAEP), suggest that the achievement gap between Black and White students has remained relatively unchanged since the early 1970s. In addition, as noted by García and Weiss (2017), the achievement gap begins early and persists throughout much of the academic experiences for many children of color.

Many researchers (see, e.g., Darling-Hammond, 1998) have explored the nature of the achievement gap between students of different racial groups, the factors that influence the gap, and solutions that eliminate the predictability of achievement by race. However, the ability to effectively lessen or eliminate the racial gap in achievement continues to elude schools and school districts throughout the United States. Schools have tried a variety of approaches: improving teachers' cultural competence, increasing student support and extending learning, encouraging teachers to vary strategies used in the class-room, focusing on school culture, and seeking additional resources (Hanover Research, 2017). Some districts will focus on one strategy, and others will roll out a group of strategies. However, there is a lack of evidence of any schools or school districts using a systemic approach to address the racial gap in achieve-ment—or that their efforts have influenced the gap in a sustainable way.

The U.S. government, similarly, has launched numerous initiatives intended to "provide all children significant opportunity to receive a fair, equitable, and high-quality education, and to close educational achievement gaps" (EveryStudentSucceedsAct.org, n.d.). These include Head Start; the No Child Left Behind Act of 2001 (NCLB; now Every Student Succeeds Act, ESSA); Title I, the National School Lunch Program; and, most recently, the White House Initiative on Advancing Educational Equity, Excellence, and Economic Opportunity for Black Americans.

Many educators hoped that the implementation of NCLB would result in narrowing the racial achievement gap. NCLB required schools and school dis-tricts to disaggregate student achievement data by race and ethnicity, ability, and language proficiency, and to make progress toward improving academic performance for all subgroups. Unfortunately, there is little evidence suggest-ing that NCLB had more than a minimal impact on closing the racial gap in achievement as measured by standardized test scores (Center on Education Policy, 2007).

ESSA was a 2015 reauthorization of the Elementary and Secondary Education Act, which was first authorized in 1965 as "the nation's national education law and longstanding commitment to equal opportunity for all students" (U.S. Department of Education, n.d.). ESSA dispensed with some of the more prescriptive requirements of NCLB while focusing on high academic standards, statewide assessments, and local innovation. Although accountability systems such as NCLB and ESSA may result in higher academic achievement overall, accountability measures alone have done little to address the racial gap in achievement (Lee & Wong, 2004).

Group-Based Inequality and Contributing Factors

The publication of *Equality of Educational Opportunity*, also known as the "Coleman report" (Coleman et al., 1966), provided one of the earliest opportunities for America to really dig into the differences in academic performance between Black and White students. This report, which was mandated by the Civil Rights Act of 1964, provided a thorough analysis of the conditions in American public schools and the barriers that prevented Black students from obtaining equitable access to high-quality schooling. Since that time, numerous studies and reports have examined the various factors that continue to lead to disproportionate academic outcomes: poverty, student culture and behavior, tracking, student mobility, lack of access to high-quality teachers, lack of culturally responsive teaching, and lack of parental involvement.

In *Dismantling Educational Inequity*, Portes (2005) approached the discussion of the achievement gap by examining how factors in schools and outside schools contribute to a predictive achievement gap, or "group-based inequality." Portes suggested that, in education, group-based inequality occurs when there is a different outcome for students who share an identifiable social construct, such as race, compared to students outside that group when all are exposed to the same instruction. According to Portes, this difference in outcome can be due to a number of factors, including a student's status or power relative to others in the learning environment, prior knowledge related to the topic, cultural context, or the student's level of development.

Examining 30 years of national achievement gap trends between White students and their Black and Hispanic peers using math achievement data from NAEP, Lee (2004) assessed factors that influence the achievement gap through three lenses:

- *Equity*—how different factors affect the ability of students to gain access to equal educational opportunities

- *Adequacy*—how the factors affect the ability of students to develop adequate levels of proficiency
- *Reciprocity*—how the factors affect the ability of students to learn in a racially integrated school

Lee concluded that there had been limited systemic improvement in any of these areas over the preceding decade and, in fact, a widening of the achievement gap. Further, Lee attributed the inability to reduce the racial achievement gap to the lack of systemic improvement in access to equal educational opportunities that would allow students of color to achieve adequate levels of proficiency and increased racial segregation of schools.

Ladson-Billings (2006) proposed shifting attention from the achievement gap to the "education debt" owed Black students and their communities. As part of this groundbreaking assertion, she delineated how this debt has accumulated over time as a result of a combination of factors (historical, economic, sociopolitical, and moral). Lozenski (2017) revisited Ladson-Billings's declaration and traced four major eras in African American education—spanning the enslavement of African people, Reconstruction, post–*Brown v. Board of Education*, and today's Black youth education crisis—to interrogate the effects of historical constructs on the achievement of Black children in the United States.

Extending Ladson-Billings's line of thinking, Chambers (2009) proposed that instead of the achievement gap, it might be more appropriate to examine a "receivement gap"—the racial gap in student achievement that results because of the structures and systems that advance White students over their Black peers. The receivement gap differs from the achievement gap by focusing on structures rather than students, as well as on inputs and not outputs. Chambers's study, which included assessing the influence of academic tracking, revealed that as early as elementary school, students experience differential treatment by school personnel that affects their later school performance. The use of the term *receivement gap* was intended to "inspire a more hopeful and nuanced discussion of the many factors that influence student achievement and distort the achievement of African American students" (p. 417).

Ability grouping (in elementary school) and *tracking* (in middle and high school), both of which involve providing instruction targeted to students' perceived capacity, also contribute to the racial gap in achievement. Schools that use these practices often see an increase in achievement for students in so-called high-ability groups and suppressed achievement for students in "low-ability groups" compared to their peers who do not participate in ability grouping or tracking (Oakes, 2005). Separating students into inflexible ability or achievement groups is associated with increased gaps in achievement overall, and studies suggest that the negative relationship between these factors is stronger the earlier a student is exposed to the practice (see, for example, Jean, 2016; Lleras & Rangel, 2009).

The continued gaps in access to rigorous curriculum and instruction are most likely the greatest contributor to racial gaps in achievement. Consider that students who are identified as low-ability in kindergarten or 1st grade generally continue in lower-ability groups through most of elementary schools, where they are less likely to have access to grade-level curriculum, which affects their ability to access honors or college-prep academic tracks once they reach middle and high school—to say nothing of AP or college-level courses offered in partnership with local universities. The impact of ability grouping and tracking extends to scores on college admission tests, the ability to obtain scholarships, and college retention and completion rates.

Garrett (2012) proposed that culture—more specifically, *oppositional culture*—also can be a contributor to racial gaps in achievement. According to oppositional culture theory, a particular social group may achieve at a lower level due to the group's disapproval of the values or behaviors displayed by the mainstream. Garrett posited that some students of color behave in opposition to expected school values so as not to be viewed as "acting White," therefore inadvertently contributing to the racial gap in achievement. Mixon and colleagues (2014) noted that African Americans' opposition to assimilation "to the perceived white culture is an important part of the educational experience of African American youth" (p. 76).

The race of school staff versus the race of students in a school—a measure of *racial congruence*—can also affect achievement. More specifically, there is a significant positive correlation between student achievement and racial congruence: the academic achievement of a Black student is positively influenced by having a Black teacher (Gershenson et al., 2022). Most students in the United States never have a Black teacher, from kindergarten to grade 12—even though teacher diversity has a positive effect on all learners (El-Mekki, 2021). This effect is even more pronounced for Black students, who are 19 percent more likely to enroll in college if they have at least one Black teacher by 3rd grade. For Black students who have two or more Black teachers, the likelihood of enrolling in college jumps to 32 percent. Black boys growing up in low-wealth communities who have two or more Black teachers on average have an on-time high school graduation rate that is almost 40 percent higher than their peers without a single Black teacher (Gershenson et al., 2022).

Teacher quality and teaching quality also affect racial gaps in academic achievement. *Teacher quality* can be defined as a measure of the possession of degree(s), teaching experience, certification, content course completion, and professional development in the content area. *Teaching quality* is a measure of the amount of time spent on basic instruction as compared to the amount of time spent on advanced instruction. Desimone and Long's (2010) findings suggested a direct relationship between the academic performance of students and the amount of time spent on advanced instruction. They also found that use of advanced procedural instruction in math and increasing the time spent on math were directly related to higher achievement for students of color and students from low-wealth communities.

Systemic and institutional racism in education is a root cause of the challenges that face BIPOC students, their families, and communities in accessing an equitable education. Creating schools that support all students—with a robust focus on equity and antiracism—requires courageous individuals within and outside the school who are willing to have tough conversations and take action.

Removing Barriers to Equity in Education: How to Use This Book

Topics of race and racism can be complex, confusing, and politically charged. This must not, however, distract us from the critical work of strategically and courageously addressing racial gaps in the U.S. education system. We must remove the barriers that stand between historically marginalized students and a great education that provides access to the hopes and dreams that they and their families have for their future.

The term *antiracism* gained popularity around 2019 with the publication of Ibram X. Kendi's *How to Be an Antiracist.* In this book, Professor Kendi discusses the difference between someone who is "not racist" (a *non*racist) and an *anti*racist, concluding that a nonracist may not be intentionally engaging in racist practices but is not really working intentionally to disrupt racism. In contrast, an antiracist is actively working against racism and the impact of historical and systemic racist practices.

According to the National League of Cities (2021), "Antiracism forces us to analyze the role that institutions and systems play in the racial inequities we see, rather than assign the blame to entire racial groups and their 'behavioral differences' for those inequities" (para. 12). The goal of this book is to provide ideas and guidance on how anyone working in public education, regardless of their specific role, can work toward dismantling systems and practices that disadvantage students of color specifically and prevent our nation from reaching its full potential.

Chapters 1 through 6 provide a roadmap that can be used in responding to racial inequities in education and creating an antiracist education system, by focusing on the curriculum, teachers, school leaders, central office staff, district leaders, and the school community.

Each chapter opens with a **trip overview**, setting the stage for the journey of its spotlighted stakeholder role and clarifying why change is needed in this particular area of the education system.

Landmarks provide examples of key hallmarks of antiracist education practice for that stakeholder role—and a discussion of how to develop them.

Roadblocks are the challenges, obstacles, and barriers the stakeholder in that area might expect to encounter on their journey toward more equitable practice.

 Shortcuts are initial quick wins and low-hanging fruit indicating ways to accelerate the process toward an anti-racist education.

 A rest stop at the end of each chapter provides a place for you, the reader, to reflect, refuel, and refresh. Working intentionally toward educational equity can be exhausting, so it's critical that you take breaks so you don't run out of gas or wind up veering off the road and into a ditch.

In the Conclusion, we discuss how to pull together the information from preceding chapters in a holistic, comprehensive way, thus increasing the likelihood that a school district will successfully reach its educational equity goals. We also suggest some action steps you can take. Finally, the Appendix shares examples of what a journey toward educational equity might look like in three districts that have different assets and are facing different sets of risks.

Getting started on this journey is as simple as making a commitment to the courageous work of equity and maintaining the sense of urgency that will keep you moving forward. Our goal is to equip you with the knowledge and tools you will need for this essential work.

1

THE ANTIRACIST CURRICULUM

What if we realized the best way to ensure an effective
educational system is not by standardizing our curricula and tests
but by standardizing the opportunities available to all students?

—Ibram X. Kendi, *Racism and the Black Experience*

 ## Trip Overview

This chapter addresses the curriculum and provides strategies to support the implementation of rigorous learning experiences that allow students of color to see themselves and their experiences, culture, and identities reflected in the content they are exposed to in schools. The curriculum, or what we teach, is a signal sender of what and who we value. Often, students of color do not see themselves reflected in the curriculum in a fully inclusive manner—or when they do see themselves and those who look like them in the curriculum, it is only through "heroes and holidays" (Rosa Parks, for example, or National Hispanic Heritage Month).

Access to a rigorous and culturally responsive curriculum where students are challenged, seen, valued, and heard can be a game changer for children of color. Access to rigorous courses is a predictor of performance on college-entry exams and a gateway to college acceptance, scholarships, and future career opportunities. When the written, taught, and assessed curricula are not aligned, educators then are in effect measuring the socioeconomic and racial demographics of a school or school district. Through antiracist curriculum, educators can create the context and conditions for all students to succeed. To achieve equitable, high-level academic outcomes for all students and prepare each student to live in a global society, it is critical that all students experience an antiracist curriculum.

Antiracist pedagogy challenges systems that perpetuate racism and categorical exclusion. Antiracist pedagogy does this is by including political, historical, and economic context in the subject matter: pushing for a critical examination of the persistence and effects of racism and racist policies and diversifying course readings and materials to include historically marginalized authors and authors with an antiracist perspective (American University, n.d.; see also University of Michigan, 2023). An *antiracist curriculum* is rigorous and culturally responsive, and fully includes the worldview of people of color—their culture, their history, and their contributions. It provides "windows and mirrors" for students of color. The mirror represents "the story that reflects their own culture and helps them build their own identity, and the window . . . offers them a view into someone else's experience" (Council of Chief State School Officers, 2019, p. 6).

An antiracist curriculum supports diverse learning styles and critiques the "hidden curriculum" of lessons that are absorbed through the experience of school: that meritocracy is impartial, that failure is merely the student's fault. The antiracist curriculum is open and inclusive of various traditions, cultures, and languages and works to reduce Eurocentrism's narrowing of the human experience and knowledge development. An antiracist curriculum includes self-reflection and societal engagement as part of the learning experience.

An antiracist curriculum does not just benefit students of color. If the curriculum is a signal sender of what and who is valued, when all students engage in a curriculum that provides a diverse (and thus more accurate) learning experience, they gain the tools and knowledge to develop cultural awareness and an antibias perspective. It is a big world out there, and the global majority is people of color. When any demographic centers their experiences, capacities, and contributions as superior, it is detrimental to society as a whole, contributing to a distorted and unhealthy worldview.

 # Landmarks

In schools that prioritize educational equity and strive to implement an antiracism curriculum, you find the following landmarks: (1) inclusivity and cultural responsiveness (i.e., diverse narratives, experiences, contributions and voices are included and valued); (2) a focus on rigor, to ensure that students are challenged to demonstrate proficiency at or above grade level; and (3) intentional probing for bias.

Inclusivity and Cultural Responsiveness

In 2000, Geneva Gay coined the term *cultural responsiveness.* In education, this means viewing students' culture and identity (including race, ethnicity, multilingualism, and other characteristics) as assets, and creating learning experiences and environments that value and empower students. There is an evolving body of research that suggests culturally responsive teaching supports student learning in a variety of ways (see Muñiz, 2019). When the curriculum is culturally responsive, "academic knowledge and skills are situated within the lived experiences and frames of reference for students"; content is personally meaningful and appealing, and "learned more easily and thoroughly" (Gay, 2002, p. 106).

A culturally responsive curriculum supports academic achievement by pushing teachers to have high and clear expectations for all students and to implement strategies to assist students in developing the academic skills needed to successfully engage in rigorous grade-level curriculum and to develop their identity as scholars. It builds cultural competence, too, by supporting educators in understanding the role of culture in education, understanding their students' cultures, and leading them to recognize their own identities and biases. Finally, it gives educators the skills to work in partnership with students to address systemic inequities in their communities and the world.

Using culturally responsive pedagogy can strengthen students' sense of identity as well as promote equity and inclusivity in the school and classroom. Teaching with a culturally responsive lens helps to ensure that all students are more deeply connected and, thus, more engaged in learning. It also supports the development of critical thinking skills. Culturally responsive teaching requires educators and school leaders to be vulnerable, acknowledging that they are not always the source of knowledge, and allows students to be experts in their lived experience and its connection to their learning and future.

An antiracist curriculum is intentional about centering the narratives, experiences, contributions, and voices of historically marginalized groups. So, how do you diversify your curriculum?

Do some research. There are many resources available online that educators can consult to help students see themselves, their culture, and their experiences in the curriculum they study. Choose those that best connect with your curricular standards and remember that people of color are not homogeneous—they represent thousands of cultures. Seek out diverse voices across ability, race, gender, and nationality.

Talk to people of color, especially if you are not one. Reach out to educators, students, parents, and community members of color and have conversations that help you to understand more about the history, traditions, and assets of their communities that you could connect to learning in the classroom. But never just contact a person of color and ask them to fill you in on what you need to know. White people looking to learn about the cultures of Black, Indigenous, and people of color too often come to or call on BIPOC colleagues or acquaintances to do the heavy lifting for them. This is not fair to BIPOC, nor is it their responsibility. Always do your own research first and show up for these conversations prepared with questions that follow up on what you have learned.

Seek to understand the lived experience of students within your classroom or your school. Talk to them. Ask them questions. Where in the curriculum do they feel seen, heard, included, celebrated, or valued? Which parts of the curriculum or learning experiences make them feel excluded, invisible, or devalued? What recommendations do BIPOC students have to make the learning more relevant to their lived experiences? Teachers, school leaders, and district leaders leaning into an antiracist journey recognize the necessity of doing this work *with* people of color, not *to* them.

Use culturally responsive teaching strategies and practices. Examples include activating students' prior knowledge, making learning contextual, encouraging students to leverage their cultural capital, and building relationships (Burnham, 2020). Encourage students to draw on their personal experiences and prior knowledge, which can be an anchor for learning. During group discussions, for example, ask questions that allow students to reflect on their lived experiences in connection with what they are learning. A curriculum that allows for the exploration of diverse topics in classrooms creates the conditions for historically marginalized students to leverage their cultural capital.

Focus on Rigor

A key contributor to the racial achievement gap is that students of color are less likely to have access to grade-level instruction and assignments than their White peers. As noted in *The Opportunity Myth* (TNTP, 2018), most students of color spend more than half of their core instructional time engaged in assignments that are below their grade level. Compared to classrooms with mostly students of color, classrooms with mostly White students average four times as many high-quality grade-level appropriate lessons. U.S. schools are failing to deliver on four key ingredients for academic success: grade-appropriate assignments, strong instruction, deep engagement, and teachers with high expectations (TNTP, 2018). These are essential ingredients in the recipe for rigor.

Many school districts continue to participate in a quasi-tracking system (see Tyson, 2013). Nationally, students of color are disproportionately enrolled in "lower ability" classes and absent from advanced placement (AP) and honors courses. Researchers have concluded that separating students into ability or achievement groups is associated with increased gaps in overall achievement (see, for example, Gamoran, 2009). Whereas students in high-ability groups experience increased achievement, students in low-ability groups experience suppressed achievement. It is not sufficient that students of color just see themselves, their culture, and their experiences reflected in the curriculum; the content must be academically challenging, and their learning experiences and assignments must push them to reach and exceed grade-level standards. So, how do you ensure students are exposed to a rigorous curriculum?

Align assignments and assessments to grade-level standards. One way to be more intentional about rigor in assignments is to frequently review student work samples and check to see how assignments align to grade-level expectations. Assignments that are below grade level are often less engaging and contribute to a decreased sense of self-worth as well as diminished interest in the subject area or school in general. If teachers are spending most of their instructional time teaching prerequisite or basic skills—depriving students of access to grade-level instruction—students will not develop the knowledge, skills, or capacity to demonstrate mastery of higher-level skills. When teachers spend most of their instructional time on grade-level content, they are engaging in one of the most important strategies in their toolbox to address racialized gaps in achievement.

Push students to use higher-order thinking skills. Asking high-level questions and giving students complex assignments require students to use higher-order thinking skills. Questions can do more than measure what students know. Appropriately challenging, engaging, and effective questions stimulate peer discussion and encourage students to explore and refine their understanding of key concepts. For example, when teachers move from asking students to memorize facts about a time in history to asking them to explain how life in that time and place would have been different if certain events had never occurred, engagement will be higher and students are likely to gain a better understanding of the concepts that the lesson is meant to convey. As another example, students could build financial literacy skills not by reading the textbook but by examining their city council's annual plans for investments to understand how their community is being invested in compared to others. These types of inquiry-based assignments stimulate discussion and creative and critical thinking, as well as reveal how well students understand key concepts.

Engage students who have learning gaps and are not yet performing on grade level. Lesson plans should address student skill gaps and incorporate scaffolds to support students in accessing grade-level content. Teachers must understand their students' current level of understanding, as the first step in scaffolding is to explain the concept and model problem solving. Then, teachers introduce new content by breaking the directions into small chunks, talking students through the task while they complete it, and allowing students to support each other through the task. In addition, teachers should provide some tips and tricks that make it easier for students to master the content.

Provide enrichment and learning extension for students who have already mastered grade-level expectations. This ensures continued engagement. There is a direct relationship between the academic performance of students and the amount of time the teacher spends on advanced instruction (Desimone & Long, 2010), which is often referred to as *teaching quality*. It means that if teachers spend most of their instruction time on prerequisite skills (below grade level), the students' academic achievement will suffer, as they will have had limited exposure to or practice with content that is on grade level. Similarly, if teachers never provide students opportunities to engage with above-grade or advanced curriculum, students will struggle to perform at higher levels. The lack of engagement with rigorous curriculum is systemically found in schools that serve students of color, and this is an area that can be addressed through teacher practice and expectation (see, for example, Tomlinson, 2023).

Intentional Probing for Bias

Implicit bias—fueled by stereotypical portrayals of people of color by the media and the lack of relationships across differences—often influences what teachers believe students have the capacity to do. When a teacher or school leader's mindset is that students of color do not have the capacity to engage in rigorous, grade-level content, those students will inevitably experience curricular tasks that are less challenging. As a result, they will not be prepared for the next grade level, let alone exposure to enrichment or gifted education.

So, how do you evaluate and offset implicit bias in the curriculum?

Audit the curriculum, instructional materials, and resources. Much of the curriculum in U.S. schools is Eurocentric—written by and from the perspectives of White people with ancestral origins in Europe. Although this is most apparent in history and literature courses, it is prevalent in almost every content area. When examining the history of the United States over the past 400 years—a time period that included chattel slavery, the removal of Indigenous peoples from their homelands, the creations of Indian schools, and Jim Crow laws mandating racial discrimination and segregation—it is easy to see the real-world effect of biases and systemic racism on BIPOC communities and important to address these truths in the classroom. However, also be mindful of the ways in which racial bias has contributed to the depiction of people of color, including their overrepresentation in subservient roles and the diminishment of their historical contributions and cultural narrative. It's essential to examine not just if BIPOC are included in the curriculum but the ways in which they are included.

Address areas where there is a lack of diverse representation in the perspectives, experience, histories, and narratives shared. Educators must question why historically marginalized people are not present in the story and then do the hard work of finding ways to ensure that those voices are reintroduced and heard.

- Classroom teachers can review the curriculum, text, articles, and other ancillary resources that are used in their subject area or grade level.
- Principals can engage grade-level teams to think about how to diversify the curriculum across the entire grade level. Teams might also audit the school's library collection and work to enrich the experiences by adding diverse voices and perspectives.
- The district's central office can lead the curriculum audit, recruiting a diverse group of teachers across the district to support this work (maybe starting with the social studies or English language arts curriculum).

 ## Roadblocks

One common roadblock on the road to implementing an antiracist curriculum is the current push to censor diverse and inclusive content—a backlash to uprisings and protests against racism and racial violence. Another roadblock is the academic curriculum itself, which is often inflexible regarding content and how to teach it.

Censoring of Diverse and Inclusive Content

Backlash to the civil uprisings and protests against racism and racial violence in the midst of the COVID-19 pandemic in the United States has included a push to limit or eliminate the use of culturally responsive curricula. In a 2022 *Fresh Air* segment, host Terry Gross noted that

> since January 2021, researcher Jeffrey Sachs says, 35 states have intro-duced 137 bills limiting what schools can teach with regard to race, American history, politics, sexual orientation, and gender identity.

Sachs has been tracking this legislation for PEN America, a writers organi-zation dedicated to free speech. He says the recent flurry of legislation has created a "minefield" for educators trying to figure out how to teach topics such as slavery, Jim Crow laws, or the Holocaust. One proposed law in South Carolina, for instance, prohibits teachers from discussing any topic that cre-ates "discomfort, guilt or anguish" on the basis of political belief (Gross, 2022; see also Sachs, 2022).

A number of school districts and even states established legislation pro-hibiting teachers from discussing social justice topics in their classrooms and districts from providing training to teachers on many equity topics. In some school districts, expectations for following the written curriculum are rigid; schools and educators are held accountable for implementing the curriculum as designed. Although there may be limits, educators can still pursue a culturally responsive curriculum while staying within restrictive curricular guidance. Teachers can create learning experiences that value and empower all students, especially those who have been historically margin-alized. They can offer learning experiences that allow all students to bring their full selves to the classroom. Students can learn in an educational envi-ronment where their culture and identity (race, ethnicity, home language) are seen as assets.

Lack of Diversity in the Curriculum

Education curricula provide guidance on the standards to be taught, but not necessarily guidance on *how* to teach those standards—and, although this is a roadblock, it's also an opportunity. Consider the different lenses content can be seen (and learned) through, such as race, culture, ability, age, and language. If those voices, experiences, or perspectives are not included in your curriculum, what articles, spotlights, reading, or audio and video resources are available that allow students to learn about the content from a diversity of individuals? For example, the English language arts curriculum standard may be that students will be able to distinguish between fact and opinion in an article; the teacher can pull together a diverse selection of articles for students to use in demonstrating this standard, selecting articles that were written by BIPOC people and content that centers the experiences of BIPOC people. Again, strive to present a variety of BIPOC voices (i.e., authors of various races, ethnicities, national origins) and a diversity of subject matter (e.g., the effect of government policies on Indigenous communities, the resiliency of Black people during post–Civil War America, the continued fight for voting rights in historically marginalized communities).

For many school districts, budgets are getting tighter, making it more challenging to purchase new culturally responsive curricular resources. If you lack the funding for new resources, explore alternative paths. For instance, a teacher can add a read-aloud to a lesson, reference an article or graphic, or include summaries, narrative highlights, and pictures in a PowerPoint presentation. Teachers can even create their own culturally responsive readers, assembling local stories from their students' communities.

 ## Shortcuts

There are several shortcuts that educators can take on the journey to an antiracist curriculum.

Classroom Audits

Teachers and school leaders can conduct an audit of school classrooms. Do the books, materials posted (posters, student work), and resources provide diverse representation across race, gender, and national origin? What are the gaps and thus the opportunities to be more inclusive? An audit is an important first step and provides a guide for strategic investment.

Student Voice and Choice

Teachers can provide students with more voice and choice in their assignments. For example, if the standard is the development of a persuasive essay, allow students to select topics that are of the greatest interest to them or related to issues in their own communities. One way to increase students' inquiry into the diverse contributions to specific subject areas is to have students do projects where they must select two people to highlight, one who reflects their own identity and one who does not.

Content Highlighting BIPOC

Teachers can make intentional efforts to ensure that people of color are included in the content they teach, on a weekly basis. It is important that the elevation of people of color does not just happen during Black History Month, Hispanic Heritage Month, Asian American/Pacific Islander Heritage Month, or other holidays that celebrate the contributions of historically marginalized groups. People of color have made significant contributions to every field and subject area, from literature and art to history, science, and mathematics. Educators who are focused on developing an antiracist curriculum must ensure that the contributions of people of color are not only highlighted but deeply investigated, discussed, and studied throughout the school year.

 ## Rest Stop

Curriculum is the "what" students are taught, and it is critical that all students—especially those from historically marginalized populations—receive constant signals that they are seen and valued. At this rest stop, we challenge you to reflect on the following questions surrounding curriculum:

- How can you ensure that students of color are accessing rigorous courses (honors, gifted education, AP, International Baccalaureate) at the same rate as their White peers?

- When examining student work, what evidence do you have that indicates students have access to rigorous and culturally responsive curriculum and instruction?

- How does your curriculum do more than tokenize the contributions of people of color during holidays?

- How does your curriculum positively center the voices and experiences of students of color?

- In what other ways can you—individually and as a member of a school or district team—help to diversify the curriculum and curriculum resources?

2

THE ANTIRACIST TEACHER

At the core of equity is understanding who your kids are and how to meet their needs. You are still focused on outcomes, but the path to get there may not be the same for each one.

—Pedro Noguera

 ## Trip Overview

An antiracist curriculum may be the foundation for schools and classrooms that are set up to achieve educational equity, but efforts to create equity-focused, antiracist schools will not be successful without effective teachers who understand the value of centering the needs and voices of students of color. Antiracist teachers use culturally responsive and affirming pedagogy to ensure all students develop a strong sense of belonging, connection, and integrity. For schools to thrive and ensure that such a culture of equity and antiracism is prioritized, teachers must be prepared and supported. This chapter explores the various attributes and strategies that support antiracist practices for teachers.

Teaching was once seen as the noblest profession by members of society. However, nationally, there are now teacher shortages in almost every state. Fewer people choose to study education, the salary is lower than in other professions, and many teachers feel disenfranchised as education has become more polarized and politicized. The stress of the COVID-19 pandemic did not help. There are different pathways to the classroom; teachers who might not be traditionally certified are still expected to be experts in content knowledge and instructional delivery.

Every member of the school instructional staff has an opportunity and responsibility to lead antiracist efforts. Antiracist teachers are leaders who expect to be held accountable and supported in their practice. They hold students to high expectations while never giving up on them. When students who are Black, Indigenous, and people of color (BIPOC) are taught using a whole child approach, they can thrive and reach their full potential. Antiracist teachers create brave spaces and are game changers on the journey to provide an equitable education for all.

 Landmarks

Effective teachers are vital to continuous improvement efforts that advance outcomes for all students and close gaps in racialized achievement. The antiracist teacher builds relational trust while centering the experiences of traditionally marginalized students. What key practices and qualities are necessary to support and empower students who are BIPOC? Landmarks for identifying the antiracist teacher include (1) teacher effectiveness, (2) high expectations, (3) a whole-child focus, and (4) brave spaces.

Teacher Effectiveness

Research clearly ties effective teachers to increased academic achievement (Hattie, 2015). However, Gonen (2015) reports that Black students in New York state public schools were 33 percent more likely than their White peers to have an ineffective math teacher. They were 44 percent more likely than White students to have an ineffective English teacher. Considering the increasingly segregated nature of schools throughout the United States, numbers like these are a flashing "Emergency" sign. Potential solutions range from paying highly effective teachers more to improving working conditions in urban and predominantly Black schools.

Teacher effectiveness cannot be tied directly to what college teachers attend, how long they have taught, or whether they are traditionally licensed (Opper, 2019b). Instead, effective teachers are those who have both deep content knowledge and the unique ability to reach students who are at varying ability levels. Scaffolding lessons while providing both enrichment and intervention are central elements of instruction in the effective teacher's classroom.

Measuring teacher effectiveness looks different from state to state. Most states use multiple factors to determine effectiveness—student test scores, classroom observations, qualitative data from surveys. In some states, these measures are triangulated using a value-added model (VAM; see Opper, 2019c) that attempts to create an apples-to-apples look at how much students are learning from one grade level to the next. Although far from perfect, these measures do indicate that a teacher with a high-value-added score is likely to have a greater impact on student achievement than a teacher with a low-value-added score (Opper, 2019a).

VAMs rely heavily on standardized test scores. Classroom observations play a more significant role in determining effectiveness in states not using a VAM. Again, observation tools vary and depend largely on the administrators' ability to recognize high-quality instructional practices. Components of an observation tool typically include content knowledge, learning environment, and professionalism (see, e.g., Rochester City School District's [2012] *Teacher Evaluation Guide*). Some states also highlight literacy, use of technology, and cultural responsiveness. Regardless of the tool, classroom observation alone cannot ensure that children of color are taught by the most effective teachers; what's pivotal is how such data are used to hire, retain, and place teachers.

High Expectations

No one "rises" to low expectations. Like all children, children of color need to be challenged to reach excellence, and maintaining high expectations is a strength of "warm demander" educators. In contrast to the sentimentalist, elitist, and technocrat educators we'll discuss later (see Roadblocks), educators who are warm demanders understand the value of building positive, trusting relationships. They are true student advocates. Under their leadership, quitting is never an option: they do not give up on students, nor do they allow students to give up on themselves.

Teachers who are warm demanders have an intentionally student-centered focus. They "expect a great deal of their students, convince them of their own brilliance, and help them to reach their potential in a disciplined and structured environment" (Delpit, 2013, p. 77). Warm demanders are nurturers at heart. More than that, they are deeply committed to providing each student with the education that they need and deserve.

Most important, these teachers stick with their students and encourage a productive struggle: Students work through increasingly challenging content and stay the course. Again, these teachers do not give up and don't allow their students to, either. They create "brave spaces" in their classrooms by building genuine relational trust. With what may be seen as a tough love approach, warm demanders are those special teachers that adults remember fondly as they recap their journeys to success. Many warm demanders have been lauded by former students during commencement and motivational speeches as they share memorable educational experiences and connections made with their favorite teachers.

A Whole Child Approach

Social-emotional learning (SEL) was first explored in the 1960s and gained impetus with the establishment of the Collaborative for Academic, Social, and Emotional Learning (CASEL) in 1994. It is now generally recognized that students' social and emotional needs must be met for learning to be most effective (see Weissberg, 2016).

Like SEL, a whole child approach is intended to holistically support students' learning and development, through rich learning environments and engagement. A *whole child education*

> prioritizes the full scope of a child's developmental needs to ensure that every child reaches their fullest potential. A whole child approach understands that students' education and life outcomes are dependent

upon their access to safe and welcoming learning environments and rich learning experiences in and out of school. (Learning Policy Institute, 2023, para. 2)

Effective teachers meet students where they are socially and emotionally, understanding that excelling academically *and* socially and emotionally will improve overall outcomes and gives students and their families hope to interrupt patterns of educational underachievement. A whole child approach creates space to recognize and address trauma, mental health challenges, and the lack of resources due to poverty.

Unfortunately—despite the fact that beliefs and goals have changed (Farrington, 2019)—the U.S. education system is still largely informed by the basic foundational structures developed in the 1800s and early 1900s. This system was not designed with a whole child approach in mind; it was based on biased beliefs and "research" findings about which students are capable and deserving of high-quality schooling. This is the antithesis of an antiracist, whole child approach to teaching and learning that is grounded in science and equity driven.

When considering a whole child approach through an equity lens, teachers need support from administrators—and without equity being a district priority, a single teacher's efforts will likely be challenging. Although the impact of a single teacher shouldn't be undervalued, when this approach is applied to a whole school or whole district, the results are more significant and more sustainable. Embedding clear expectations, a comprehensive professional learning plan, and strategies (to include resources or a toolkit) in the district's strategic plan gives teachers the best opportunity to be successful.

Brave Spaces

What does it mean to create a classroom environment where students can bring their whole selves? Often, teachers and leaders strive to create safe spaces in schools and classrooms where all children can thrive. But schools and classrooms should also be inclusive and equitable. Teachers who embrace antiracist practices move beyond safety and strive to create brave spaces.

To understand the difference between "brave" and "safe" spaces, consider that *safety* implies that no harm will be done, and neither the environment nor the practices will cause harm. This is important. Every student should feel safe while at school. *Bravery* is not the absence of fear; it's showing physical, moral, or emotional strength in the presence of fear. A brave person risks action even when afraid or unsure of the outcome. Creating brave spaces is about creating conditions that allow students to take risks as learners.

In brave spaces, under the teacher's leadership, members of the class work to accept the fact that they may sometimes feel uncomfortable and at times defensive. Despite these feelings (or, better yet, because of these feelings), the classroom culture is judgment-free and supportive. Students have the space to feel, unpack, and reflect on their emotions. Authentic relationships are built by understanding shared experiences.

Stubbs (2019) outlines a framework for brave spaces based on six pillars: vulnerability, perspective taking, leaning into fear, critical thinking, examining intentions, and mindfulness. Brown (2012) defines ***vulnerability*** as uncertainty, risk, and emotional exposure. When teachers and students give themselves permission to be vulnerable, their efforts consciously create a classroom environment that is conducive to deeper engagement.

We all see others and situations through our lived experiences. Teachers and students do not need permission to own their perspectives. Brave spaces honor others' **perspectives**. This allows students (and teachers) to remain curious as they seek to understand their peers.

To "**lean into fear**," teachers and students should practice doing things that make them nervous or afraid. Brave spaces provide a supportive space to lean into fear rather than avoid it. Doing so helps to reframe how the brain views fear, creating opportunities for growth.

Critical thinking includes deep questioning and being open to critique without feeling attacked or defensive. Students and teachers in brave classrooms ask thoughtful questions and expect the same of others.

Examining intentions means checking and understanding boundaries and striving to be self-aware of one's own intentions. In the antiracist classroom, teachers and students consider how their words and actions affect others. In brave spaces, they question whether their messages are received as they expected and whether their contributions further the dialogue.

The final pillar, **mindfulness,** is about staying in the moment. This is especially helpful when engaging in difficult discussions. Practicing mindfulness both allows space for the other pillars and encourages focusing on the present rather than allowing inner chatter to distract.

Brave spaces center student voice. Teachers can ask each student to define *brave* and share their definitions and examples with others, either as a class or in small groups, or share a common definition of the word to begin the conversation. Classroom expectations developed collaboratively are then based on agreed-upon key practices, and classroom routines are aligned with the pillars of brave spaces.

Further, students should explore the concept of bravery based on their own experiences. Students might write about or reflect on a time when they felt brave. What caused them to feel brave? How did it feel to be brave? What images, thoughts, and feelings come to mind when they think of feeling brave? Students can also use art by illustrating this feeling. Through a combination of whole-class, small-group, and one-to-one discussions, each child should be encouraged to share and discuss their feelings of bravery.

As this process develops, students might use journals or sticky notes to record their thoughts and feelings. This information helps the teacher to lead more discussion and support the class in developing a social contract, poster, pledge, motto, or other guidelines that inform classroom beliefs and norms. Complete classroom guidelines should be created collaboratively. These may include the six pillars as well as showing the kind of respect to others that you expect to receive, assuming good intent, being a risk taker even when it's uncomfortable, and listening actively, especially when it is something difficult to hear.

Brave spaces allow for and invite students to bring their whole selves into the classroom. Moving beyond "safe" and into brave spaces gives teachers and students an environment that lends itself to open and authentic engagement that builds and enhances relationships.

 ## Roadblocks

In establishing an antiracist classroom, teachers can face many challenges and roadblocks. There are no simple solutions or a one-size-fits-all protocol.

Self-assessment of mindset is crucial, as is remaining steadfast and open to creative solutions. Common roadblocks include low expectations for students who are BIPOC, sentimentalist or technocrat teachers, and elitist teachers and leaders.

Low Expectations

Low expectations from school or district leaders for students who are BIPOC can make this work especially difficult. In a best-case scenario, the principal and leadership team are guiding responses to the challenges that accompany creating a culture of equity. Lacking such guidance, teachers should lead from the seat they are in while seeking allies within their own school and other schools in the district, region, or beyond. When encountering someone who has lowered expectations, consider "calling in"—offering support and thought partnership—rather than calling others out, which can cause embarrassment, shame, and hostility and lead to fractured relationships. You cannot be responsible for someone else's inability or unwillingness to grow, but you can gently nudge them forward by calling them in. There is no magic formula to change mindsets or to shift expectations from low to high. Sharing data, having candid conversations, and demonstrating a willingness to partner in this work are great places to start. Be open-minded and understand that getting to equity and antiracism is a journey, not a destination. People travel at different paces and via different routes.

Sentimentalist, Technocrat, and Elitist Teachers and Leaders

Traditionally marginalized students do not need sympathy. Yet "sentimentalists" tend to make excuses for students who perform below grade level. They allow classroom behaviors that may be detrimental to student success. With a sense of warmth and often the best intentions, these teachers and leaders allow students to give up rather than engage in productive struggle. This interaction results in having low expectations that harm children who are BIPOC and prevents them from excelling. Although students often like sentimentalist teachers, these teachers are pushovers and do students no favors. Good intentions only go so far. Children of color need teachers who care enough to hold them accountable for learning at high levels.

Sentimentalists do care about their students, and the nurturing that they provide is important, especially for children who have experienced trauma or who live in a consistently traumatic or unsafe environment. However, these educators miss the fact that a high-quality education could very well be what saves the life of such students. Not supporting students in mastering grade-level standards will most likely result in limited opportunities and more stress and trauma as an adult. Learning is not always easy, even for the most supported, well-adjusted, and thriving students. In fact, learning can be a challenge for both children and adults. Recognizing that it is acceptable and expected that there will be struggle at times and being prepared to support, encourage, and inspire students to keep going can make a difference in academic outcomes.

From a distance, "technocrats" appear to be the best of the best. Competent in their subject matter and enthusiastic about learning, these teachers seem smart and capable. They hold students to high standards and expect them to meet them. Yet they provide little support, and although they may be likable and liked, they do not explicitly strive to build rapport with students.

Technocrat teachers could be described as mastering the science of teaching yet falling short on the art of building relationships. Like sentimentalists, they mean well and do not intend to cause harm. Technocrat teachers and leaders are most comfortable with students who are independent learners, leaving dependent learners feeling well-liked but still not learning at a level that will lead to mastery.

Elitist educators always maintain a professional distance and view students who are different—racially, culturally, linguistically, and socioeconomically—through a deficit lens. Low expectations are allowed, as is off-task behavior (as long as it is not disruptive). Elitist teachers often operate from the mindset of "I got my education, and it's up to you to get yours" or "Only the best students should get a high grade in this class, so I need to make it as challenging as possible and provide limited support." Elitists think that it is the students' responsibility to learn, and any student who *doesn't* learn is at fault. To this end, scaffolding—a strategy for supporting learners by building background knowledge and filling in knowledge gaps that keep students from accessing the content—is not included in their teaching repertoire. Specific strategies to engage struggling learners are seldom seen in a classroom taught by an elitist teacher.

These teachers keep students at a distance and do not pursue meaningful relationship development. In fact, they have little or no desire to develop relationships with people (children or adults) who differ from them. Students tend to view elitist teachers as cold, unfriendly, and uncaring.

Elitist teachers and leaders may present the most challenging roadblock. Viewing children through a deficit lens is counterintuitive to equity and antiracist practices. Individuals can only "change" themselves—and that change happens from within. When encountering elitist educators, model the characteristics that have proven to be effective in engaging children who are BIPOC. As when creating brave spaces, changing one's own elitist mindset requires a level of vulnerability that can be uncomfortable. An elitist must be willing to ask and answer tough questions around how they feel about children who are BIPOC and why they feel that way. They must be willing to challenge their own beliefs, which may have stemmed from their upbringing, experiences early in their career, or even mentors or leaders with whom they have worked.

 ## Shortcuts

Overcoming roadblocks can be challenging, yet effective teachers identify the "low-hanging fruit" that can make a difference in the short term.

Build Relationships

Understanding your own relationship-building style can help overcome the barrier of not being a natural warm demander. Not understanding this or being in denial is a major roadblock. Read, research, and study with a partner teacher to develop characteristics that are conducive to building and sustaining positive relationships with students. In schools with an established coaching community, this can be done by partnering teachers of different styles with one another. Team teaching and side-by-side coaching may prove effective in sharing instructional approaches as well as exploring relationship styles. As appropriate, include students in discussions to learn more about why they may feel more of a connection to some teachers over others. This should be done in a brave space where students can be authentically truthful with no fear.

Be a Leader

This may not sound like a shortcut, but consider how teachers view one another. What is the culture of your school, of your grade level or content area? What do other teachers need that you can provide? You can commit to being a leader without being appointed as one. Undoing hundreds of years of racism and oppression of historically marginalized groups requires everyone to be an equity leader. Lean in hard.

Reach Out to Alumni

Learn more about the education experiences of your alumni who are BIPOC. You can do this by using various social media networks or by inviting alums back each year to share their experiences with your students. Such visits could be done routinely throughout the year as well as at key times like PTA meetings, homecoming, prom, and graduation.

Create a Student Advocacy Group

Student leadership organizations tend to attract students with drive, confidence, and experiences of succeeding in school. When setting up a student advocacy group to advance equity, look to recruit a new set of less conventional leaders—students who may have sat on the sidelines due to shyness, a passive personality, behavioral challenges, or even grades. Suggest that school leaders use a broader focus and an equity lens for selecting student leaders who can inform school direction. Use your voice and ask key questions such as these:

- How can we center the experiences of students who have historically not thrived in our schools (as demonstrated by limited academic success, high rate of absenteeism, or frequent suspensions)?

- How can we center the experiences, needs, and passions of students who are not thriving?

Rest Stop

For schools to thrive and ensure that a culture of equity and antiracism is prioritized, they need effective teachers—and these teachers must be supported and empowered to find and use their voice. Antiracist teachers are effective: They have exceptional content knowledge and understand the importance of high expectations. Being relational and warm demanders, they intentionally create brave spaces that allow children of color to bring their full selves to the classroom. At this rest stop, we challenge you to reflect on your practices and your roadblocks. There will be school staff who may not see the point of equity and antiracist practices. Call them in rather than calling them out. Having a mutually respectful relationship will make this easier. Here are some reflective questions and tips that may help:

- What student and achievement data might raise awareness? Invite your colleagues to be thought partners in identifying root causes, specifically looking at ways that school, classroom, and district practices negatively affect student outcomes and brainstorming actionable solutions. Do you have data that reflect the effects of successful strategies to address the needs of BIPOC students and families? What practices can be replicated and deepened for even greater impact?

- What is your "why"? Share your why with clarity and ask colleagues to do the same. Join a social media group (or start one); social media offers many opportunities to engage with equity leaders throughout the country and the world.

- How are you currently giving your students a voice? What more can you do to center their experiences? Ask them about their hopes, dreams, challenges, fears, and what they need from you as their teacher. Ask them to describe an ideal teacher. Make it fun and use art. Be intentional about striving to meet their needs and creating brave spaces.

- How are you taking care of yourself? Being an antiracist and a champion for equity are not without challenges. Burnout is real and can be inevitable if you're not practicing self-care. Begin with the basics, such as getting enough sleep and some physical activity. Further, set aside time to decompress in the evenings; this might include journaling or just turning off technology 30 minutes before bed. Having an accountability partner in your wellness practice may increase consistency and even make it enjoyable. Teaching can be socially overwhelming, so being proactive by planning self-care will help.

3

THE ANTIRACIST SCHOOL LEADER

*Accountability is hard for adults, but a lousy education
is calamitous to children for the rest of their lives.*

—James Comer

 ## Trip Overview

The success of a school is largely dependent upon the effectiveness of the school leader. School leaders are among the most influential stakeholders within a school district. They shape the culture and climate of their school; their leadership is paramount in ensuring that students who are Black, Indigenous, and people of color (BIPOC) receive the education that they deserve. Antiracist school leaders support teachers and staff in removing barriers while providing brave spaces where students can thrive academically and socially. They are student centered and understand how to lead with data when sharing the compelling "why" of equity and antiracist work.

Leading equity and antiracism work demands focused and committed school leaders who are prepared to understand, respect, and serve their community.

It is the responsibility of schools to provide not only a well-rounded, rigorous education for all but also a safe, nurturing learning environment that supports each child's whole self. By the time children who are BIPOC enter kindergarten, many are already feeling the social and cognitive effects of racial bias, trauma, and poverty (Pumariega et al., 2022). School leaders must be prepared to create and support student-centered learning environments that are both culturally responsive and center each student's sense of safety and connection.

 ## Landmarks

School leaders who prioritize antiracism and equity in education approach challenges from a student-centered perspective and use strategies that support this priority. Landmarks for such leaders include (1) building positive school culture and climate, (2) supporting brave spaces, (3) providing intervention and enrichment, and (4) interrogating racialized data.

Positive School Culture and Climate

There is a large body of research regarding the influence of school leader effectiveness on positive student achievement and outcomes. Educational equity and antiracist work, like any other changes, are best received and implemented when the culture and climate are positive.

Fullan (2007) defines *culture* as the guiding beliefs and values evident in the way a school operates. This includes the attitudes and expected behaviors of teachers and students, and it ranges from how children are treated to how decisions are made. The National School Climate Center describes school *climate* as the "quality and character of school life" (2007). Although the terms *culture* and *climate* are often used together or synonymously, they are not the same. Both are important in any school setting—and without a robust school culture and climate, other strategies are not likely to succeed or to be sustainable.

There are many benefits to having a productive school culture and climate. Among the most vital are improved academic outcomes and increased feelings of safety. Culture and climate create a foundation for supporting antiracism and equity in education.

Valuing teachers and staff. Principals establish positive, productive school cultures and climates by valuing teachers and staff, affirming the history and traditions of the local community, and selecting teachers and staff who support equity and antiracism. As Connors (2000) warned, if you don't "feed" the teachers, they will "eat" the kids. School leaders are responsible for ensuring that teachers are fed. One way to do this is by sharing clear expectations—ideally, ones that the teachers helped to establish. After all, teachers feel the direct effects of districtwide and schoolwide decisions and changes. Including teachers and staff as collaborative team members when decisions are being made demonstrates that their knowledge and experience are valuable and that their needs matter.

Quality feedback gives teachers a greater understanding of their areas of strength and for growth. When performing a teacher observation, the school leader should share feedback within 24 hours along with next steps for supporting needs or exemplars. For example, a teacher may excel in making learning relevant to her students' lives but need support with transitioning between activities. In our experience, teachers who complete targeted and relevant professional development activities and see their revised practices translate into student achievement gains feel both valued and valuable (see Will, 2017). Happy teachers are better teachers.

Teachers are the boots on the ground for equity and antiracism work. Valuing them by including them is necessary for success. Building positive, sincere relationships makes this work more enjoyable and tangible.

Valuing community and diversity. Schools are microcosms of their communities; effective school leaders understand, respect, and include the community. Supporting community traditions and cultural norms goes a long way in establishing a school as the center of the community. Representation matters in each classroom of every school. Children of color are more likely to thrive when they have at least one teacher who looks like them (Gershenson et al., 2022).

Schoolwide Brave Spaces

In addition to a worldwide pandemic, the year 2020 also brought to light the racial injustice that has plagued our nation for centuries. The killing of George Floyd and other unarmed Black people sparked national and global outrage. Many children of color experienced racial trauma because of these events, compounding the effects of the pandemic on their families while learning remotely. This added to trauma that already existed in the lives of many of our youth. These unprecedented circumstances of increased trauma have heightened the need for school leaders to prioritize emotional safety. One way to do this is to create brave spaces where students and staff can have conversations about trauma, poverty, and race and the effects that each has on learning.

As discussed in Chapter 2, educators readily acknowledge that schools should be safe places; the challenge is to move from safe to brave spaces. The key to creating brave spaces is to include (and work to center) the voices of those most likely to be silenced or go unheard. Fostering a culture of trust and inclusiveness is an important step for school leaders on the journey toward antiracism and equity in education.

Brave spaces in classrooms and schools allow students and staff alike to feel safe, respected, and included. For the traditionally marginalized, this means gaining voice and choice—and seeing their experiences and culture normalized. Within diverse groups, all members should feel safe. School leaders set the tone for and drive the kind of culture where this kind of safety is expected.

Amplifying staff and student voice. As when establishing classroom brave spaces, creating a schoolwide brave space first requires discussion: your school community must define *brave* and ensure clarity. Every member of the school community should have a voice in this discussion. School leaders guide the discussion, with questions and prompts that inform efforts at the schoolwide level:

- What makes you feel safe?
- Share a time when you did not feel safe.
- What does it mean to feel brave?
- What do you need from your school to feel safe and brave?

Students and staff who are BIPOC need opportunities to converse and collaborate in both homogeneous and heterogeneous groups. There is a comfort level associated with being with members of one's own identity group, racial or otherwise. Conversations surrounding brave spaces can be very personal and cross lines; it can be more difficult to share and dare in this way within a mixed-identity group. School leaders must understand and be prepared to lead and model courageous conversations.

Establishing conversation norms and guidelines. Establishing conversation norms—ones like "Speak your truth," "Assume good intent," "Ask for clarification when you need it"—helps to avoid classroom microaggressions and misunderstanding while encouraging active listening. The more members of the classroom community who buy into these norms, the more perspectives will be heard and respected. And you're most likely to get broad buy-in when norms are established collaboratively, with input from teachers, staff, and the students themselves.

Conversation guidelines provide a social contract between all members of the class and school. Like conversation norms, conversation guidelines should be established collaboratively among teachers and staff and students. The intent is to highlight what is valued in the class and school, and what is not acceptable. Examples of conversation guidelines include "Work hard not to be defensive even if someone challenges your ideas" and "Even if you are unsure or uncomfortable, participate and take a risk." School leaders, while encouraging some autonomy and room for creativity, must also ensure that norms and guidelines consistently support the overall school culture.

Brave spaces should be representative of the school community and each classroom. One of the easier ways to do this is by displaying culturally relevant and personally meaningful artwork in various locations throughout the building. Encouraging students to create story maps and self-portraits to post in the learning spaces helps to increase their senses of ownership and belonging. Brave spaces affirm the belief that every student and staff member is valued—inclusive of race, ethnicity, sexual orientation, religion, and other unique factors.

Interventions and Enrichment

Brave spaces are a starting point in establishing student-centered schools. Student-centered schools focus on how actions of adults affect students. Leaders in these schools encourage active consideration of student outcomes, needs, and interests as decisions are made. Many go a step further and include students in decision making, which demonstrates that the school sees their scholars as individuals with valuable viewpoints and thoughts (Sudderth, n.d.). Effective school leaders ensure that students have access to both necessary interventions and enrichment, and they use an equity lens to identify and remove barriers to success.

Providing effective interventions. Before identifying specific supports, school leaders must establish the "why." This is imperative for making decisions that best support students. School leaders should know and be responsive to the needs of their community (e.g., effects of trauma and poverty). Selected interventions should be evidence based and vetted to ensure that they focus on assets and don't do further harm to historically marginalized students and families. Remember, the purpose of intervention is to address gaps in knowledge or skills necessary to reach grade-level proficiency, not to lessen the expectations.

Providing access to enrichment. Gifted and talented education programs—the "other segregation" (Pirtle, 2019)—sometimes divide schools and create separate but unequal education systems within a school or district. Academic and racialized tracking further limit which students receive acceleration and enrichment activities. Nationwide, Black students make up about 17 percent of the student body, yet fewer than 10 percent are identified as gifted and talented. In contrast, an overwhelming 53 percent of students who receive remedial support are Black (Pirtle, 2019).

School leaders who are serious about providing equitable opportunities for all students must examine the policies, practices, and perceptions that limit access. For example, if the goal is to increase the number of BIPOC students in advanced classes to a percentage that reflects the school's racial demographic, there must be an intentional focus on the admission criteria. Be aware, too, that when Black students are selected for gifted programs, they may feel isolated if few children of color are included in such programs. In an antiracist school, adults ask, "What changes do we need to make to change the experience for our students? How are we building the scholar identity of our BIPOC students?"

It's important to remember the long-standing stigma attached to Black students being smart. BIPOC students being accused of "acting White" for enjoying reading or earning high grades should not be tolerated. Note, too, that very smart students of any race are often ostracized (Desmond-Harris, 2017). Shifting this paradigm requires that leaders stress the beauty and benefit of being well educated while also ensuring that policies and practices are aligned to recognize giftedness in BIPOC students.

Leaders must examine each aspect of the criteria for admittance to gifted programs and advanced classes through an equity lens. Further, recognizing that representation matters, school leaders should be intentional about hiring BIPOC teachers and providing the support necessary to retain them.

Interrogating Racialized Data Through an Equity Lens

In schools that are student focused, leaders must ask tough questions regarding racialized data points and boldly interrogate the wide variety of data that inform policies, procedures, and practices. *Interrogating data* means asking the right questions, using the right data, and relentlessly giving a voice to traditionally marginalized students. An *equity lens* helps to shine a spotlight on any student group that has been underserved. This means focusing on the gaps that exist for English learners (nonnative English speakers); students with learning differences; and those who are underresourced due to geographic location (inner-city and rural students), race, or ethnicity.

School leaders must use all available data points to prioritize student needs—including direct input from students. Whether through surveys, conversations, or direct observation, it's essential to empower students to express their hopes and dreams as well as what they need from their school to inform the outcomes and direction of their education journey.

School leaders focused on instilling a culture of equity ask tough questions such as:

- Does this policy or decision adversely affect already marginalized students?

- Have we intentionally involved all stakeholders who will be affected by the decision?

- How are we collecting and using data to determine the effectiveness and success of this effort? What data are we collecting that inform the effects on students who are BIPOC?

- Have we identified potential barriers to success or access and considered how to eliminate or minimize them?

- What resources are allocated to ensure that teachers and staff are equipped to implement this action?

In addition to removing barriers, effective school leaders institute a framework for student support and advocacy. *The Road to Student Success: A Toolkit for Student-Centered Advocacy* (National Education Association Center for Advocacy and Outreach, 2015) is one comprehensive action guide aimed at implementing and advancing a student-centered agenda. The guide presents a team approach to strategic planning and includes steps for SWOT (strengths, weaknesses, opportunities, and threats) analysis, action planning, and evaluating the work.

 Roadblocks

School leaders are charged with supporting and advocating for all students. Clearly defined equity policies and frameworks make this work less complex. In many schools and districts, particularly those with a majority BIPOC population, equity requires the removal of barriers and increased advocacy efforts aimed at improving social, emotional, and academic outcomes.

Identifying roadblocks prior to or early in the journey will help make a smoother road trip. The challenges will vary from school to school, and educators who prioritize equity and antiracist practices should prepare to stay the course. Remain steadfast and open to creative solutions. Some common roadblocks include a lack of systemic practices, fixed mindsets (on the part of both educators and students), and resource deficits.

Lack of Systemic Practices to Support Equity

One roadblock is when a school district has neither a strategic plan for nor a focus on equity. The best remedy is to take a leadership stance by identifying what other, effective districts do and making a case for updating or developing a strategic plan that prioritizes equity and antiracism. School leaders who are a part of the district leadership team are best positioned to do this. Still, whether explicitly on a team or not, school leaders play an important role in shaping and informing district outcomes. They are uniquely positioned to support and provide insights to the superintendent, chief of schools, and other influential leaders. If this type of bold leadership does not work or fit, school leaders can seek allies from other schools, outside and within the district, and among community leaders. An ally can act as a sounding board or thought partner and may also be able to suggest tangible solutions based on their own experiences. Allies in this work honor humanity and can help push work forward when there are gaps in systemic planning.

Fixed Mindsets

This is the most common roadblock and applies to most aspects of this work. Effective leaders do not have fixed mindsets, but at some point, they will encounter staff and other stakeholders who do. In this case, their leadership is imperative.

As previously discussed, academic tracking can create a school within a school. A common consequence is the routine exclusion of students of color from programs and classes that promote advanced learning (Education Trust, 2020), often attributable to implicit bias and systemic racist practices and policies. When leaders are working to change educator mindsets and increase access to rigorous curriculum for students of color, one approach is to share why equity matters in the lives of the children being served. Be specific in sharing examples of when a focus on equity and antiracism improved specific student outcomes, and lean hard on the most compelling data points. Then appeal to the heart by encouraging those you're speaking with to ask themselves, "Is this the education that I would want for my own child?" Modeling what is expected is important; teachers and staff should be able to *see* the equity and antiracist leadership in their school leaders.

In many high school classrooms across our nation, advanced classes are disproportionately the realm of White students. Why is that? Peer pressure is widely seen as a student influence that may overpower parental and school expectations (see Kellogg Insight, 2018). In the Black community, the accusation of "acting or talking White"—using standard English, reading a book, or being interested in advanced studies—may be a deterrent to some Black students behaving in a scholarly manner (Tyson et al., 2005). Few would deny that education is a key to individual success and to improving family and community economic, social, and health outcomes. Antiracist school leaders must interrogate this phenomenon if they suspect it is a barrier for their BIPOC students.

Resource Deficits

The resource deficits school leaders often face—both financial and staffing-related—can introduce detours to the journey.

Partnerships are frequently required to bridge financial gaps. As part of the comprehensive school planning process, a needs assessment can help determine the resources a school will need to reach its equity goals. And note that those resources should be directly tied to the budget. In addition to partnership, also consider how federal funds or other financial resources might be applied. Write grants, seek volunteers, and join others who are doing this work. Create coalitions or join an existing one. Identify local or national nonprofit organizations that focus on equity, antiracism, and social justice. Look for free resources and opportunities aimed at supporting schools. School leaders should be intentional about establishing and strengthening partnerships that can provide professional development and other needs.

 Shortcuts

Addressing antiracism and equity in education presents both challenges and opportunities for school leaders. Although there is no singular easy path and advocates must be prepared to do the work, there are some clear approaches that can be implemented for quick progress. Prioritizing antiracist practices is necessary, and you can do it by committing to low-risk, high-impact strategies.

Build Relationships

Model relationship building by greeting students by name and using positive and affirming language, every day. Addressing students by name makes them feel valued and seen. Support teachers in intentionally creating spaces for relationship building within their classrooms—a reading corner, an area for hands-on learning and collaboration—that are comfortable, inviting, culturally responsive, and age appropriate.

Provide Space for Wellness

In addition to collaborative spaces, encourage teachers to provide space for emotional regulation for their students. Think of this as a wellness and self-care center with calming music, age-appropriate coloring books, and manipulatives. Students should be partners in creating this space.

Similarly, prioritize adult self-care. A schoolwide wellness team could identify an area—consider replacing the traditional teachers' lounge—where adults can have a time-out to focus on their mindfulness. Consider creating an environment of mutual respect between adults and students: Does your school have an open area where all school members can convene? Could you repurpose a computer lab or carve out a space in the media center for this purpose?

 Rest Stop

Establishing a culture of equity and antiracism requires committing to a student-centered approach to education. Understanding the needs and challenges of the students being served highlights the need for equitable, antiracist practices and policies. Students who are BIPOC disproportionately experience trauma, poverty, and segregated school conditions that impede their success. To create a student-centered, antiracist school, leaders must prioritize building a positive school culture and climate, creating brave spaces, providing interventions and enrichment, and interrogating racialized data.

At this rest stop, we challenge you to reflect on the following questions and ideas surrounding school leadership:

- How does your leadership support school culture in providing brave spaces for your students and staff? What more can you do?

- What do your students need to feel supported, and what more can you do to advocate for them?

- If your school does not have an equity leadership team, establish one to interrogate data using an equity lens, and create a school-level equity plan.

- Consider establishing a wellness committee to develop supports for students and staff.

- What student-centered data sources should be interrogated within your school? Seek input from students to learn more about their experience in your school.

- How are you taking care of yourself? School leaders are often faced with stressful responsibilities and unrealistic expectations. Work to maintain a mindset that focuses on what you "get to do" rather than "have to do." For example, you *get to* support teachers who will influence the lives of hundreds of young people. You *get to* be a part of a community of learners who can influence the entire city, county, district, division, or parish. What else do you get to do as a school leader?

4

THE ANTIRACIST
CENTRAL OFFICE TEAM

---

*Let us put our minds together and see what
life we can make for our children.*

—Sitting Bull

 Trip Overview

This chapter reflects on ways that the various positions in typical district central offices can support an antiracist, equitable education for all students. Central office staff play an essential role in providing systems, structures, and support that enable districtwide transformation. They help to establish baseline expectations, provide foundational support, and can ensure equity across schools by providing strategic support where the greatest needs exist.

Antiracist central office teams align their resources to the district's strategic priorities, addressing these through an equity lens. This alignment, an important signal-sender to schools, can be managed through messaging, professional development offerings, and personnel and nonpersonnel resource investment. Although these functions may go by different names—"teaching and learning" versus "curriculum and instruction" or "human resources" versus "employee services"—the main functions are similar.

An antiracist central office team can build a foundation of excellence and equity, working collaboratively across departments to maximize their influence. This central office team ensures that the district maintains high expectations and provides the resources and support for those farthest from opportunity. Over time, antiracist central office teams create the conditions that eliminate racial disparities in students' outcomes and allow students, staff, and families not only to reach their full potential but also to access the hopes and dreams they have for the future.

To lead a district's antiracist education effort, the central office team first must understand why equity is important and essential. Having a shared understanding of the "compelling why" builds constructive collaboration for antiracist work. Central office teams should develop a refined equity lens (see the discussion in Chapter 3) that enables them to take both collective action and individual action—examining, for example, their own identities and mindsets and how their individual actions might move the school district toward more equitable outcomes.

The central office team may need time to build their knowledge regarding the history of race and racism and its effect on all systems, not just education. They may need to build skills to work collaboratively across teams to develop policies and systems that create the conditions for action that leads to equitable outcomes. They must know and be able to describe what culturally responsive teaching practices are (see Gay, 2000) and have expertise in interrogating their own biases and those they encounter in their work.

 ## Landmarks

Antiracist central office teams view all components of their work through an equity lens. For these teams, equity is front and center, not an afterthought. Central office teams that support the schools in their district in closing equity gaps exhibit landmarks in specific areas: (1) data and accountability, (2) teaching and learning, (3) community engagement, (4) communications, (5) student support, (6) human resources, and (7) budget and finance.

Data and Accountability

The data and accountability team (or individual) within the central office typically collects, disseminates, and analyzes data elements such as standardized test scores, attendance, grades, enrollment, and teacher quality. There are many data metrics that schools and school districts collect that can provide insight to equity gaps. Do student achievement outcomes differ on the basis of race, language, or any social construct? Can the assignment of high-quality teachers be predicted based on the demographics of the student population?

Disaggregating data. The collection and monitoring of data disaggregated by race, ethnicity, ability, and home language is key to antiracist work and is essential when assessing challenges and the root causes of racial disparities and determining the effect strategies and investment may have on closing gaps in student outcomes. Most school districts gather data on attendance, discipline, standardized test scores, grades, promotion rates, course enrollment, and student perception. They also gather data such as demographics by school, teacher quality, funding per school, funding per program, and service hours for students with disabilities. Each data point, when disaggregated by race or other social constructs, provides valuable insight to the steps a district needs to take on its antiracist journey to equity. The analysis and monitoring of data allows a district to assess which strategies are working and which are not. The central office data analysis team can identify and highlight bright spots or positive outliers that could be studied further to uncover unique gap-covering strategies that might be replicated and scaled up at other schools.

Developing and monitoring district goals. Improving student outcomes is strategic work. Antiracist data accountability teams can support the district's strategic plan as well as individual school improvement plans through the creation of SMARTIE (strategic, measurable, ambitious, realistic, time-bound, inclusive, and equitable) goals. SMARTIE goals enable the district or school to identify strategies and action steps; the central office team can support this effort by monitoring data points to determine if selected strategies are affecting the metrics.

The identification of *inclusive and equitable* goals is critical: when goals are inclusive, historically marginalized people are intentionally brought into the work or process and involved in decision making in a way that clearly demonstrates that power is shared. Such goals clearly address systemic injustice, inequity, or oppression; for example:

- Reduce the gap in the identification of Black boys for special education services as compared to their peers by 10 percent annually for the next three years.

- Reduce the racial gap in enrollment in AP/honors math classes in high school by 15 percent.

This work helps to ensure that antiracist strategies are embedded in the district's strategic plan and school improvement plans. The central office team can identify actions and resources that will support the current goals that will lead to more equitable outcomes.

Interrogating factors that contribute to racial inequities. The antiracist data and accountability team works to find or create metrics that enable greater insight as to the effect of strategies and resource and personnel investments. They may gather and analyze data such as placement of high-quality teachers, for example, to determine if teacher quality might be a factor contributing to low achievement for some schools. Providing data regarding shifting demographics at a school could support community engagement teams in preparing for the effect of such trends on school communities. Evaluating programs focused on supporting boys of color might reveal whether the attendance, academic performance, or behavior data for students in such programs improve compared to their peers of color who do not participate.

An antiracist data and accountability team also supports the district and schools in presenting data to the community. They ensure that the information shared is accurate, user friendly, and accessible—and that the data describe both the closing of gaps and overall improvement. Frequently providing the community with data can be an important strategy for trust building. Connecting the data to strategies and the budget helps stakeholders understand why specific investments are prioritized. Antiracist data and accountability teams use data to build the compelling reason for getting to educational equity.

Teaching and Learning

In Chapter 1, we discussed the purpose of and need for an antiracist curriculum. Curriculum is *what* is taught; instruction is *how* the curriculum is taught. Students' classroom experiences have an immense influence on outcomes and on closing racial achievement gaps. The central office's curriculum and instruction team (or individual) supports teaching and learning through evaluating and identifying curriculum resources, offering differentiated professional development, and providing support and resources.

Supporting implementation of a culturally responsive curriculum. Curriculum and instruction teams lead the district's development, acquisition, and implementation of a rigorous, culturally responsive curriculum and identify complementary instructional materials aligned to grade-level expectations. They understand the state curriculum requirements and standards; review and procure district curriculum resources; and provide guidance on the use of supplemental resources, including learning scaffolds and extensions. Antiracist curriculum and instruction teams ensure that the needs of the historically marginalized students are centered when making decisions about developing or purchasing curriculum resources. They thoroughly review curriculum resources to ensure that

- BIPOC students and their communities are positively and equitably represented;
- The narratives shared about BIPOC are comprehensive and speak to their diversity, contributions, and history; and
- The curriculum supports positive racial identities and social justice.

Providing professional development. Antiracist curriculum and instruction teams provide differentiated training to instructional staff (i.e., coaches, teacher supervisors, teachers) on what high-quality culturally responsive teaching and learning look like. They differentiate training to ensure that the professional development offered supports staff throughout the journey of becoming an antiracist educator, whether staff are at the novice, developing, or expert level. They ensure that the teachers in their district and new teachers coming to their district receive foundational equity and antiracist trainings that interrogate the district's understanding of race and racism and its effect on education, the role that bias plays in the educational experiences of students who are BIPOC, and how teachers can establish culturally responsive and affirming educational environments where all students thrive.

Offering support systems and resources. Antiracist curriculum and instruction teams understand that getting to equity in education is a journey, and one that requires continuous development and support. They examine systemic structures to ensure that all staff who interact with students have the skills and knowledge to ensure that every student is seen, valued, and challenged. This includes establishing professional learning communities (PLCs) to support teachers in leading their own development with their peers. They ensure that principals and instructional coaches have resources that enable the evaluation of equitable and culturally responsive teacher practices. Antiracist curriculum and instructional teams develop, curate, and maintain a collection of rubrics, model lessons, and videos that provide guidance on what high-quality culturally responsive instruction looks like.

Community Engagement

The antiracist central office community engagement team (or individual) views families and the community (see Chapter 6) as asset-rich allies whose engagement, partnership, and support are essential to getting to equity. They lead from the point of view that families and the community must be engaged in the development of the district-level strategic plan and school-level improvement plans, and they must be at the table when solutions for tough equity challenges are being worked out. As such, antiracist community engagement teams are strategically positioned to support stakeholders in leaning in from an equity lens.

Identifying community partners. Community engagement teams are essential to building support for a district's or school's antiracist work. These teams often have the role of mining for community partners who can support the district's various needs. They typically have a good sense of what partners are in the community and those partners' priorities. Antiracist community engagement teams use their knowledge of community assets to identify specific partners and resources to meet the district's equity goals. In identifying equity-aligned partners, antiracist community engagement teams research community organizations and build bridges between the district's needs and the community organization's goals. For instance, community engagement teams may be helpful in identifying partners who could support expanding leadership and college access programming for boys of color. Antiracist community engagement teams work to ensure that community partners are aware of the district's equity vision and support these partners in identifying ways that they can, in turn, support the district's antiracist and equity goals.

Engaging families. Antiracist community engagement teams also provide schools in the district with strategies and resources to engage families and to build their own partnerships based on the specific needs of the school and its community. A district that receives Title I funding and whose students qualify for free and reduced-price lunches is required by law to "explain how it will promote parent involvement" (EdPost, 2021, para. 11). Oftentimes school staff lack the skills to effectively engage parents and families in low-wealth communities or those that historically have experienced harm or had limited success with public schooling. Antiracist community engagement teams bridge relationships between historically marginalized communities and their schools. It's work that begins by adopting an asset-rich mindset and striving to connect—authentically and intentionally—with students' families. High-functioning and antiracist community engagement teams provide schools with the resources to build families' capacity to support and advocate for their children's education needs and to lean into leadership roles in their schools.

Providing equity-focused resources. Antiracist community engagement teams are adept in providing resources and strategies to deepen engagement with families and the broader school community to ensure that historically marginalized voices are centered in discussions and decision making. In addition, operating through an antiracist lens, community engagement teams provide foundational training and equity-focused resources to families and community partners to support their understanding of race and racism and its influence on their communities and, specifically, schooling. They work to build parents' ability to effectively advocate for the needs of their students and to engage in solution building for the equity challenges their schools face.

Communications

One role of the central office staff is to facilitate the conversation surrounding the district's equity priorities and strategies for improving student outcomes. Robust communication strategies are essential for building positive, trusting relationships with stakeholders, including staff, students, families, school board members, and the wider community. The antiracist communications team (or individual) supports the district in articulating its "compelling why"—the story of why its equity work is important—in a way that is personal and relatable to every stakeholder.

The antiracist communications team also ensures that the stories the district shares include representations of its diverse school staff, students, and parents. They highlight contributions across communities, socioeconomics, race, and culture. This team is intentional about ensuring that boys and young men of color are recognized for academic contributions, not just athletic ones, and that Hispanic or Indigenous students are recognized year-round, not just during heritage celebrations.

Another important role of an antiracist communications team is to support schools when responding to incidents of hate and bias, by providing templates to support thoughtful and transparent communications about tough equity issues. In this effort, the central office's communications team is essential to getting to educational equity.

Providing user-friendly messaging. The antiracist communications team develops materials in students' and their families' home languages that tell the story of the district's equity work. This messaging—in a variety of voices and formats (articles, presentations, videos)—includes specific examples of what equity work looks like in schools and the community. Effective teams create structures that allow the team to quickly respond to feedback from various stakeholder groups. User-friendly messaging is essential to creating the conditions for families and students to be advocates.

Telling the story of equity work. Antiracist communications teams can create toolkits that school leaders can use when talking about the effects of the district's equity initiatives at the school level, helping schools to share stories of how this work has made a difference in the lives of individual students. Because equity work can be political and volatile, it is important for the communications team to stay in front of the conversation and support the district in effectively telling its own story. Communities can get "stuck" on a single idea (e.g., that focusing on supporting historically marginalized students somehow results in other students getting less), and unless the district's communications team is providing counternarratives, the support for the district's or a school's equity work can be derailed.

Student Support

The central office's antiracist student support team (or individual) helps create the conditions under which vulnerable students and families can thrive. In the United States, students of color are overrepresented in most at-risk categories, including high poverty (Boschma & Brownstein, 2016), homelessness (Gonzalez et al., 2021), non-English proficiency (NCES, 2019a), and almost all learning disability categories (NCES, 2019b). Effectively supporting students of color is essential to eliminating racial achievement gaps—and antiracist student support teams go further, to ensure that the district intentionally implements actions that center the needs of students of color.

Implementing a multitiered system of supports (MTSS). MTSS (see Harris, 2020) is a well-known framework for providing timely, strategic, and evidence-based academic and social-emotional support to ensure all students thrive. Antiracist student support teams evaluate interventions for bias and evaluate data trends in the MTSS by race, achievement level, and home language. They make sure that MTSS support plans start with an analysis of student strengths and interests and include the identification of a "school champion"—a staff member committed to establishing a positive relationship with the student and ensuring their success.

Antiracist student support teams recognize that educator mindset affects teacher performance (the rigor at which students are engaged) as well as student experience (what students believe about themselves as learners). Therefore, in the high-quality MTSS systems that they implement, antiracist student support teams make sure supports and interventions are available for teachers as well. These range from training, modeling, and coaching to ameliorate instructional gaps to antibias training and assessing a school's learning conditions and current supports for students of color. The overall goal of the teacher-focused support is to ensure all staff believe that *all students* are capable of successfully engaging in high-level learning, have the skills to support each student's success, and that teacher mindsets don't get in the way of achieving educational equity.

Meeting the needs of at-risk students. The student support team focuses on providing additional resources and supports to meet the needs of students furthest from opportunity: students with disabilities, gender-nonconforming students, English language learners, students and families experiencing homelessness or housing transitions, and students living in low-wealth communities. The antiracist student support team understands the intersectionality of race and other social constructs, such as socioeconomics, disability, homelessness, gender identity, and language proficiency, and it pursues the specific, targeted support needed to remove barriers that are unique to historically marginalized student groups. Rather than simply compiling a list of supports, they look for evidence that the supports have positive effects and are actually effective in reducing racialized student outcomes.

For example, a district has food pantries at its schools for students experiencing food insecurity. The student support team, evaluating the effects of the program, learns that students are not accessing food because they are embarrassed to be seen with the green food-pantry bag. The program is tweaked to stock pantries with plain paper bags and allow students to use bags brought from home. They also learn that families don't like the food selection, so they ask for feedback on the list of offerings and invite families to come in and shop in the pantry themselves.

Another district's student support team has been conducting research on how the district's McKinney-Vento funds and other resources might remove barriers for students living in transitional housing. One key barrier they identify is that these students face transportation challenges in accessing academic support at school, so they institute a tutoring program based at the homeless shelter and work with community partners to provide ride-share tokens and public transportation vouchers.

Addressing student trauma. Antiracist student support teams focus on supporting emotional well-being. They understand the connections between stressors (e.g., poverty, violence, economic instability) and learning. These teams prioritize creating the conditions in schools that calm the brain and create a strong sense of belonging for every student. Student support teams leaning in through an antiracist lens focus on the implementation of trauma-responsive supports, such as creating developmental relationships and supportive environments. More important, antiracist student support teams acknowledge the significant effects of racism and racial trauma on students and staff and create resources, training, and strategies to mitigate the effects. They provide training and supports to school-based mental health practitioners that increase practitioners' skills surrounding racial trauma, and they lead efforts to destigmatize accessing mental health services in communities of color and find ways to engage youth in this work.

Developing nondiscriminatory discipline practices. Students of color are disproportionately referred for school discipline, including exclusionary practices such as in-school suspension and out-of-school suspension (Chen, 2023). These disproportionate referrals contribute to the overidentification of boys of color for special education services on the basis of emotional disability (Morgan, 2020).

Student support teams, leaning in through an antiracist lens, examine discipline data disaggregated by race and work with schools that have racialized gaps, interrogating discipline trends to identify the root causes. They then support schools through training and implementing alternatives to exclusion to move toward more equitable discipline outcomes. In addition, at the district level, these teams work to clarify and limit law enforcement involvement to dangerous, violent behavior. They work to decriminalize age-appropriate, inappropriate behavior and support schools in implementing restorative and trauma-responsive practices to create the conditions for all students to thrive and learn.

Human Resources

Schools are the unit of change for the district, and teachers are the unit of change for the school. The antiracist human resources team (or individual) at the central office understands that sourcing, hiring, and retaining a high-quality, diverse teaching staff that reflects students' communities is key to addressing racialized gaps in achievement and, ultimately, to district- and school-level success.

Placing highly qualified staff at schools with the greatest needs. To counter the trend of students with the greatest needs being taught by teachers with the least skill and experience (U.S. Department of Education Office for Civil Rights, 2014c), districts can provide incentives to place and keep the best teaching and educational support staff at schools with the greatest needs. Such incentives could include early contract offers, signing or relocation bonuses, or reimbursements for licensure exams.

Implementing training and pipeline programs. Providing high-quality onboarding programs for new teachers and educational support staff ensures that new hires quickly come to understand the district's equity priorities. As part of onboarding experiences, the antiracist human resources team provides opportunities for new staff to understand the district's commitment to culturally responsive and rigorous education and to learn about the rich history, assets, and challenges of the communities that they will serve. Establishing pipeline programs or "grow-your-own" programs (see Garcia et al., 2022) is a way to diversify teaching talent from within (see also Chapter 5). Many such programs also provide a supportive pathway for instructional support staff (e.g., teaching aides)—many of whom live in the surrounding community and have strong positive relationships with the students—to obtain teacher certification.

Budget and Finance

Central office budget and finance teams (or individuals) have incredible opportunities to influence the ways that school districts direct funding. It is their responsibility to identify needs and support districts in meeting them. Antiracist central office budget and finance teams work to ensure that the students and schools furthest from opportunity receive the resources and supports they need to catch up and keep up.

Leveraging funds to provide strategic support. Title I and other Every Student Succeeds Act (ESSA) funds can be used to invest in evidence-based practices that have demonstrated success in closing outcome gaps for historically marginalized students. There are also other federal grant programs (see, e.g., AtRisk Youth Programs, 2023) for which schools may be eligible. Antiracist budget and finance teams implement differentiated funding models that allow funding to support the most at-risk students. In addition, teams can provide grant-writing and funding proposal support (i.e., federal/state grants) to schools to increase access and opportunity for historically marginalized student groups.

Supporting bond referendums for capital project planning. Capital improvements can help schools in BIPOC communities with a history of underfunding get to equity. Antiracist budget and finance teams help the district and community stakeholders better understand the gaps in funding that often keep schools in historically marginalized neighborhoods from receiving adequate support for facility maintenance and upgrades. They help to lay out long-term plans that lead to more high-quality schools, regardless of location and student demographics.

 # Roadblocks

Central office staff play a key role in realizing a school district's antiracist vision and strategic priorities surrounding education equity. However, there can be roadblocks on this journey, including a lack of alignment of priorities within the office and a lack of skills and knowledge on the part of individual staff members.

Lack of Alignment of Priorities

Historically, the work of central office staff is conducted in silos, where each team's or individual's priorities are separate and distinct. This can be a significant barrier to advancing a district's antiracist vision. When there is a lack of alignment and clarity on the district's priorities and their intersection with antiracism, work might be labeled "equity work" or "antiracist work" but not result in any change in student outcomes. One way to address this roadblock is to ensure that there is a clear vision for the antiracist work and that the district's leaders stamp the priorities, actions, and resources that will be invested to support the work. Many districts do this by establishing an equity or antiracist vision and mission statement or creating equity and antiracist policies. Creating a district policy makes it more likely that all stakeholders will be clear on the district's vision for equity and how it plans to get there.

Lack of Skills and Knowledge

When the antiracist work is stuck, it is important to ask whether the team lacks the *skill* or the *will* to do the equity work. If it is a skill issue, the central office team needs training to build their knowledge and expertise regarding antiracist and equity work. This training should clarify what the district specifically means about "getting to equity." Formal foundation training is important, as are opportunities for central office teams to build their skill and alignment related to how their team can affect racial student outcomes. It is also essential to provide learning opportunities in smaller and more intimate settings that promote authentic and brave conversations. This might include brown-bag lunch chats for central office staff or within a specific central office team, as well as opportunities for staff to connect with system leaders.

 # Shortcuts

Robert Frost's line "The only way out is through" is often quoted to encourage staying the course when work is difficult. However, there are some strategies that antiracist central office teams can implement to accelerate progress toward antiracist goals without a significant investment in time or finances.

Build Relationships and Commitment

Central office staff members need to build relationships with each other and with school and district leaders to enable them to talk vulnerably about the challenges being faced. Team members need trusting relationships within which they are not afraid to say, "I don't know" or "I feel differently about this idea." Sharing stories from school leaders, staff, parents, students, and the community about how equity work is transforming lives can help build commitment to the mission and vision. A series of meetings between district leaders and central office staff teams to talk about the effects of equity work can help to highlight the role of individuals and teams as well as provide an overall orientation to how the district is approaching the challenges of getting to equity.

A series of foundational training courses for central office staff, similarly, helps to get everyone on the same page. Content might include the effects of systemic racism on education and education systems, and strategies that are being used effectively to undo the resulting harm. Connect the equity work that staff members are already doing and plan to do to the district's strategic plan. Teams and individuals already monitor certain data metrics; illustrate for staff how to use an equity lens within this work, looking at racial gaps and aligning strategies to address challenges.

Celebrate Wins

Celebrate your wins, even when they are small. Antiracist work is hard, and sometimes it can seem that opposition and obstacles exist on every side. It is critical that teams take the time to appreciate wins, even when they are small. Celebrate team members who are showing up authentically and courageously taking risks in your antiracist work. Remember, what is celebrated is a signal-sender about what is valued.

 Rest Stop

At this rest stop, we encourage you first to reflect on and celebrate your own commitment to antiracist work—and that of others in your school and district. There are always early adopters and like thinkers—who is already leaning in through an equity lens? Create and support your coalition of the willing. We encourage you to refuel; take time to invest in yourself and your team.

We also challenge you to reflect on the following questions:

- How are the actions of your central office team aligned and mutually reinforcing toward the district's equity goals?
- What data are you using to monitor student outcome gaps?

- What is the effect of central office team work on students and families who are the farthest from opportunity? How does your school or district budget prioritize support for its most vulnerable students?

- Do your actions, strategies, or policies further exacerbate racialized gaps in student outcomes?

- How are you prioritizing "gap-closing" strategies?

- Where are the gaps in understanding and knowledge? What type of professional development can you offer to build expertise?

5

THE ANTIRACIST
DISTRICT LEADER

---

*Not everything faced can be changed, but
nothing can be changed until it is faced.*

—James Baldwin

 ## Trip Overview

Although every position in a school district is important, there is no denying
that the district leader's influence is most crucial to improving outcomes
for BIPOC students. Effective equity leadership requires a focus on systemic change that is intentional and data driven, and that clearly specifies
expected outcomes. There are several key steps that, when done well, lead
districts toward a destination of equity and antiracism. Successful district
leaders must set a clear vision for equity defined and developed through a
strategic plan. Such leaders must be intentional and establish clear and high
expectations aimed at improving academic and other outcomes for all students. In addition to focusing on the whole child, leaders must also employ

a whole educator approach when consistently striving to improve school and district culture.

The antiracist district leader values and is unapologetic about having clear and high expectations for teachers, leaders, and staff. Superintendents—or, in some districts, chancellors, administrators, managers, or chief executive officers—set the tone and are the filters for improvements and change within their schools and community. They ensure support for their cadre of teachers and other employees through a whole educator approach. Achieving equity in education is a journey; district leaders are key to navigating and overcoming the roadblocks that can make for a bumpy ride. Antiracist district leaders are essential in staying the course.

 ## Landmarks

District leadership is a must for a successful antiracist journey. Improved outcomes for students who are BIPOC are dependent upon effective, equity-focused district leadership. Key landmarks for the effective antiracist district leader include (1) having a vision for equity, (2) maintaining clear and high expectations, and (3) focusing on the whole educator.

A Vision for Equity

When school boards seek a new superintendent, inevitably they look for a visionary leader. Some go as far as to include the term *equity focused*. District leaders must have a vision and be intentional about ensuring that vision is a shared one. For districts striving to be antiracist and achieve equity in educational outcomes, this vision is imperative.

Setting a vision for equity, like other priorities, is best done through a robust strategic plan. According to a veteran superintendent on the West Coast, "a strong strategic plan is essential in carrying out equity work. A solid strategic plan clarifies the priorities of the district and the broader community through the initial engagement process when the plan is created" (personal communication, April 10, 2022). The first step to including an equity focus in the strategic plan begins with establishing definitions and expressing the "why."

Defining the focus. In partnership with the school board and a diverse body of district and community stakeholders, superintendents lead the conversation by clarifying the need for equitable antiracist practices. As described in Chapter 4, this can be supported by interrogating racialized academic data and identifying the root causes of existing achievement and opportunity gaps. Gaps may be tied to barriers that limit access to rigorous teaching and learning (Darling-Hammond, 1998; Education Trust, 2020); if so, *equity* might be defined as removing barriers while providing access to rich, culturally responsive teaching and learning to all students. Antiracist district leaders and their teams also consider the intersectionality of race and other factors, such as home language, gender orientation, disability, and socioeconomic status to ensure that strategies are sufficiently nuanced to meet the real needs.

Identifying and embedding core values. The strategic plan should specify core values that are aligned with an equity and antiracist approach. *Core values* are the characteristics or traits that are deeply valued and represent the driving force to inform the work of the organization. For the antiracist district leader, equity is a core value that is elevated, clearly defined, modeled, and celebrated.

After collaboratively identifying four or more core values, leaders must work with internal and external stakeholders to ensure that the values are embedded in the culture and expectations for each school, department, and work group. Each value must be defined, along with tangible examples of what it looks like in the lives of students. Integrity, for instance, might be defined for students as well as adults and then intentionally included as part of character education and within a variety of content areas. Posting core values throughout the organization is a nice touch but only if they are real and visible in how children and adults are treated within the school community.

Linking expectations to policies. Deep equity work has a greater opportunity for success when expectations are policy driven. A clear vision for equity can lead to a board-approved equity policy solidifying a district's dedication to providing educational equity (see, for example, Howard County Public Schools, 2020). Such a policy might include equitable hiring practices, systemically using disaggregated qualitative and quantitative student and workplace data, raising the measured achievement of all students while narrowing achievement gaps, and graduating all students ready to succeed in the workforce and/or postsecondary education. The policy and its supporting procedures are also an opportunity to call out and lift up specific groups such as Black male students who have been traditionally marginalized. Ultimately, a high-quality equity policy aims to eliminate the predictable, disproportionate academic, social-emotional, and disciplinary outcomes based on students' race or ethnicity, gender, language, poverty, and special needs.

Assessing equity and inclusion. A final aspect for establishing a vision of equity requires remaining data driven. Conducting an equity and inclusion assessment is an important step to this end. A business owner and professor in Kentucky who has conducted comprehensive equity assessments for over two decades describes this assessment as

> an examination of the existing [organizational] culture with emphasis on equity, inclusion, and diversity. The assessment examines the institution's strengths and deficits with respect to ensuring that students have the opportunity to be academically successful. (Personal communication, April 10, 2022)

Equity and inclusion assessments address areas such as diversity, academic disparities between BIPOC students and their White peers, disproportionality in special education identification and student discipline, opportunity gaps, recruitment and retention rates (of BIPOC and other employees), access to diverse faculty and staff, and climate and culture. This in-depth process provides multiple data points that superintendents and district leaders can use to make informed decisions regarding the most strategic ways to move toward more equitable educational outcomes. Through a combination of a desk audit; classroom observations; stakeholder interviews; and online diversity, equity, inclusion, and belonging (DEIB) surveys, the detailed report is an invaluable resource for monitoring equity outcomes. Research and evidence-based recommendations can also be provided, along with support for implementation of a district DEIB plan inclusive of professional development and instructional resources and aligned with the district's strategic plan.

Clear and High Expectations

With a strong strategic plan that includes meaningful core values, district leaders are poised to share the needs and expectations of the community as they seek high-quality talent. Hiring the best, most effective teachers and leaders is one of the most important roles of a superintendent. With no end in sight to the national teacher shortage, this has become increasingly challenging. Successful district leaders are creative. They build leadership pipelines, understand cultural competence, and focus on hiring teachers and leaders who are the best fit for their organization.

Building an effective leadership pipeline. This effort begins by establishing clarity around district leadership needs, which can be done formally with an aspiring leaders' academy that prioritizes understanding district culture while improving student outcomes. By aligning academy modules with district strategic plan areas (i.e., equity and antiracist goals), superintendents position future school leaders to be successful and ready to lead. Such an academy is not just a principals' training ground. Teachers, instructional coaches, counselors, and others should be encouraged to attend even if they choose to remain in their current roles.

Leadership pipelines do not stop once team members assume leadership roles. Effective superintendents create robust professional learning communities where principals and other leaders are supported using a coaching model. For example, the Inquiry Cycle Tool (University of Washington Center for Educational Leadership, 2022) guides leaders in analyzing evidence of student learning and teaching (and leading), developing an action plan, and then analyzing the effectiveness of the plan. Antiracist superintendents can use such a framework to personalize professional learning to support district goals.

Valuing cultural competence and perspectives. An Alabama superintendent who serves in the Black Belt region believes that high expectations must include actively valuing students who are BIPOC and understanding them from a cultural perspective. As she told us, "In order for children of color to bring their whole selves into the classroom, the classroom must be a community that values and reflects children of color in the visuals, materials, library books, and instructional content and discussions" (personal communication, April 10, 2022).

School leaders and teachers must learn cultural competence to ensure school environments, classrooms, and instruction are culturally responsive, relevant, and equitable. Moreover, before culturally responsive, relevant, and equitable schools and classrooms can be realized, leaders and teachers must learn about themselves, their roots, beliefs, and values; gain an awareness of other cultures; and acknowledge and accept differences in appearance, behavior, and culture that differ from their own.

Hiring and onboarding. Hiring forward-thinking teachers who are the best and brightest goes a long way toward establishing schools with a clear equity focus. District leaders must be clear about this during recruitment and hiring. Potential employees should be able to tell, from the district website and social media outlets, that the district prioritizes equity and antiracism. Further, the interview process should be intentional and designed to eliminate candidates who would not be a good fit.

Once hired, leaders must ensure that teachers have the support and professional learning they need to be successful. All new teachers should receive a comprehensive plan for professional development early in their tenure—one that includes the district's areas of focus (from the strategic plan) and offers opportunities for personalization.

A Whole Educator Approach

Just as effective teachers take a whole child approach to education, district leaders must prioritize the whole educator. A senior leader from the Midwest told us that this "begins with an action-oriented ethic of care for people who you want to be their best for children. An action-oriented ethic of care means as a leader, you see the person before you see the position they hold" (personal communication, April 12, 2022).

The whole-educator focus is compassionate, empathetic, and supportive, without disempowering teachers' ability to see their own expertise and worth. When leaders clearly demonstrate an ethic of care that is actionable, they learn about district educators as individuals—which in turn helps them to better understand what educators need and how they function collectively. This process builds the social and emotional intelligence of educators and leaders, creating conditions that cultivate respect.

Increasing collective teacher efficacy. The whole educator approach is a school and district culture builder that leads to increased collective teacher efficacy (CTE)—a staff's shared belief that, through their collective action, they can positively impact student outcomes, even for those who are disengaged and most vulnerable (Fisher et al., 2016). CTE is ranked as the number one factor influencing student achievement, with an effect size of 1.57—more than three times as powerful and predictive of increased student achievement as socioeconomic status, and more than double the effect of prior achievement (Visible Learning, 2023).

Respecting staff and responding to their needs. Compassionate, empathetic leaders must have a genuine respect for the challenges that teachers, leaders, and staff face. Discussions surrounding public education are increasingly polarized and politicized (Houston et al., 2022). District leaders must provide a buffer for their team members while establishing inclusive opportunities for their voices to be heard.

In practice, this means going beyond simply adding teachers to a committee to listening and acting upon their stated needs. Superintendents should sincerely ask teachers what they need with the intention of striving to meet their needs. There should also be an opportunity for follow-up, to share progress and evaluate the success of processes. This can be done by conducting teacher-inclusive before- and after-action reviews of new processes. A *before-action review* examines the proposed process and asks the questions "What will success look like?" and "What could go wrong?" It's a forum for teachers to add their perspective to these issues, which allows leaders to begin with the end in mind and some of the key hazards already identified. An *after-action review* examines the completed process by asking, "What went well?" and "What would we do differently?" Both kinds of action reviews can be expanded with additional questions and personalized to improve effectiveness.

The antiracist district leader understands that teachers, leaders, and staff must be in environments where they feel valued, respected, seen, and heard; this is the cornerstone of the whole educator approach. Essential components include recruiting, supporting, and retaining effective BIPOC staff; a strong DEIB focus and policy; and districtwide practices that support DEIB.

 **Roadblocks**

Every school district has its unique challenges. Superintendents must know their community in order to quickly respond to roadblocks such as fear of change, misunderstandings surrounding equity and inclusion, and teacher resignations and staffing shortages.

Fear of Change

Fear of change can thwart equity efforts before they have time to blossom. Equity work requires courageous leaders. Exploring how to get comfortable being uncomfortable with equity work can help, but leaders must have the fortitude to keep going. To that end, leaders must not subscribe to the ideology that "it's lonely at the top." Being a lonely leader is a poor choice for leaders on a journey toward equity and antiracism. Colleagues who are engaged in the work make great thought partners—as do champions of this work in other fields. Be open to learning from others.

Change is hard and can evoke reasonable fear. Equity leaders must be prepared to handle the pushback that may ensue, while holding true to their belief that all children deserve a high-quality education. Connecting regularly with colleagues or mentors is one strategy. Another is to write about the experience of being a champion for equity. This can be in the form of a blog or op-ed for public consumption, or simply a journal for self-expression. Writing about one's experiences can be a powerful tool for decompressing and gaining perspective.

Finally, leaders must take care of themselves, physically and emotionally. Enjoying family and friends and engaging in a hobby are helpful. Fear is natural. Leaders must be courageous and stay focused on their goal.

Misunderstandings About Equity and Inclusion

Critical race theory (CRT) is an academic and legal framework that describes systemic racism in U.S. society. Public and political opposition to and misunderstandings about CRT can create distractions and barriers to equity work.

There are those who target equity, social-emotional learning, and culturally responsive teaching as aspects of CRT, with the goal of quashing discussions surrounding racism.

Superintendents are responsible for protecting their teachers and staff from unwarranted accusations; they also have the responsibility of educating the public about what is being taught in schools. It is important to work with legislators to continually clarify the need for equity in education and to be courageous enough to share a compelling "why." Having a healthy relationship with state legislators can go a long way toward creating an understanding of what equity and antiracist work looks like and to clarify the purpose and need.

Addressing this roadblock starts with having one-on-one meetings with members of the state legislature. Every state except Hawaii has a state administrators association, which is affiliated with the School Superintendents Association (formerly known as the American Association of School Administrators [AASA]), an organization that can provide a seat at the table and a collective voice that state legislators will hear. The work done conducting an equity and inclusion assessment provides data to discuss with local and state leaders. Lift up the voices of BIPOC students and alumni. What was their experience in school, and how could it have been improved?

The "Great Resignation" and Teacher Shortages

Since spring 2021, an elevated rate of U.S. workers quit their jobs amid strong workforce demands associated with the COVID-19 pandemic. The "Great Resignation" hit school districts especially hard, exacerbating long-standing teacher shortages. Staffing challenges can create additional stress and have a negative impact on school and district culture. Leaders must be proactive in addressing this. A strong recruitment and retention plan that includes "growing our own" leaders builds a pipeline of future teachers and leaders and partnerships with local and regional colleges and universities. Further, being intentional about improving working conditions for all employees elevates and supports a positive and robust school and district culture. This cannot be a "one and done" approach; it requires ongoing efforts to attract and retain talent.

Shortcuts

Superintendents are in a prime position to look for quick wins as they dive into equity leadership. Keeping in mind that the work must be collaborative, leaders who understand how to support the whole educator while being creative in recruiting and retaining talent will find themselves on the road to success.

Celebrate Staff Members

Establish a districtwide reward system that celebrates teachers, leaders, and staff who embody the district's core values and focus on equity. Partner with the community to provide winners with gift cards, duty-free lunch periods, or opportunities to lead and highlight their talent as district exemplars. At the culminating end-of-the-year event, roll out the red carpet and give teachers celebrity treatment!

Share Successes and Address Challenges

Create or encourage teacher-led groups that provide safe spaces and "think tanks" to share successes and seek support for challenges. Coordinating with a fellow superintendent to create inter-district groups would further expand the idea pool. These teacher-led groups could meet to conduct a social media chat, participate in a statewide Webex meeting, or access a discussion group through a learning management system. Jointly presenting at a regional or national conference would make a great culminating activity. Those who want more might even create a podcast to deepen connections and expand the reach of the work that is being done.

Expand Partnerships in the Community

Effective partnerships can expand options and access for students who have been furthest from opportunity. Starting with career and technical education classes, leaders can expand partnerships with nearby schools of education to create a "future teachers association." Secure funding to support tuition payments; students in the program agree that, upon graduating, they will work in the district for a certain number of years.

Rest Stop

Creating an antiracist school district where equity in education is prioritized requires courageous leaders who can engage stakeholders. At this rest stop, we challenge you to think systemically about what might make for a smoother journey toward an antiracist school district.

- How clear is your district's vision in terms of supporting equitable and antiracist practices? In what ways is the vision seen in your work? What gaps need to be addressed?

- Do district hiring practices and policies result in employing diverse, effective talent who believe all students are capable of learning at high levels?

- How do your district and school leaders support the whole educator? What more should be done to ensure that teachers' voices are lifted up in a meaningful way?

- How much do you know about your state legislators, especially those who set legislative priorities that affect equity work? Who are the gatekeepers, and how can you engage them?

- Who else is focused on equity and antiracist work? Who in your state or region is doing similar work, and what are their results? How do they engage their local communities and connect with local allies?

- How are you taking care of yourself? Leading a school district can feel lonely and isolated, so self-care and wellness are imperative.

6

THE ANTIRACIST COMMUNITY

A child who is not embraced by the village
will burn it down to feel its warmth.

—African Proverb

 ## Trip Overview

This chapter reflects on ways that the broader community can align to support schooling that produces excellent learning outcomes that are not discernible by race. Any person or team engaged in leading equity work within their sphere of influence is an equity leader. Working in solidarity with all equity leaders—whether students, family members, business owners, leaders of non-profit organizations, or faith leaders—is key to becoming an antiracist community.

Communities can leverage their collective power to push for the equitable allocation of resources, time, and talent so that the greatest disparities are addressed. It will be difficult, if not impossible, to significantly and sustainably eliminate racialized education outcomes without comprehensive investment from the community. Engaging with school boards and elected officials is essential to addressing equity gaps and creating a platform that prioritizes equitable student outcomes. There are strategies community leaders can use to prioritize eliminating opportunity gaps in their communities, including aligning priorities and resources across multiple sectors such as safety, health care, housing, foster care, policing, employment, and food security.

In many school districts in the United States, stakeholder feedback has led to the establishment of equity offices and to funding of diversity, equity, and inclusion staff positions. The establishment of educational equity initiatives, task forces, and committees reflects concerns communities have expressed regarding disparate outcomes for or treatment of those who identify as Black, Indigenous, and people of color. Students, families, and members of the community all have unique perspectives and assets that can be strategically leveraged to address inequities.

Strong community relationships should be a pillar of the antiracist approach in every school district. However, three key things are necessary if these relationships are going to make a difference in changing disparate student outcomes:

- School districts must be vulnerable enough to transparently and frequently share data, as well as strategies for monitoring student outcomes.

- School districts must be willing to share strategic development and decision-making power with the community.

- School districts must prioritize the needs of historically marginalized populations.

 ## Landmarks

When school districts have the support of an antiracist community, racialized gaps in student outcomes can be narrowed and even eliminated. Communities that see diversity as a strength are key to achieving equity in education. Antiracist communities understand that investing in schools and creating the conditions for all students to reach their highest academic potential is not just a financial game changer for students; it's a financial game changer for the community, too. Landmarks for such communities include (1) supporting student advocacy and agency, (2) empowering families to lead systemic change, (3) engaging partners with culturally specific expertise, (4) leveraging support from elected officials, and (5) establishing a community-led equity committee.

Support for Student Advocacy and Agency

Students are the first and most important stakeholder group to engage on the road to becoming an antiracist school district and community; their lives are the ones most significantly affected by school decisions. Ensuring that every student receives a high-quality education is critical to our nation's future, and students have valuable insight into the current education system and its challenges. Students are an incredible asset in creating an antiracist community. When students have agency and voice in their education, they are able to help solve complex equity challenges.

Students can provide evidence of what is really working in a school and what is not. Their input can help school staff and leaders to get to the root cause of culture and climate issues and other school challenges, such as why a particular course has significant high-failure rate for BIPOC students. Communities that are leaning into becoming antiracist provide brave spaces for student voice (see Chapters 2 and 3) and advocate for student agency and the freedom for students to be engaged in decisions about their own education.

Engaging students as co-creators of solutions. Many districts and schools already have student groups that they leverage to provide input to decisions. It's important that these student groups are diverse by design to ensure that the needs, interests, and concerns of all students—especially those who have experienced less success in schools—are considered. Communities can also create opportunities for students to lead as part of a city or community youth council, a youth advisory group to the school board, or a youth council connected to other community organizations (e.g., the National Association for the Advancement of Colored People [NAACP]) that specifically support the needs of historically marginalized communities.

Engaging students as co-creators of equity solutions requires the continuous interrogation of power dynamics. Are students' ideas and recommendations being considered equally? Are students really co-creating, or are they being given the opportunity to provide feedback or input? Productive conversations and interactions are structured in a way that allows all stakeholders to apply an equity lens (i.e., examine gaps by social constructs such as position, age, race, gender, ability, home language, and socioeconomic factors). An equity lens pushes individuals and teams to consider who benefits from decisions and who does not. Antiracist communities prioritize the application of an equity lens and ensure that it guides both discussions and subsequent decisions.

Building students' leadership skills. Our students have unique talents and gifts waiting to be awakened and developed, but they also have lots to offer right now. They can contribute to a better and more equitable community even when they are very young. For example, even students in the elementary grades can lead service learning projects in which they identify a school or community need and then research, propose, and implement a solution. However, to be equity leaders in their school and community, they may need to build their equity skills; one way to do this is by participating in equity training, either monthly or during the summer. Youth equity trainings can be co-developed with students, school district staff, and community partners, with the goal of encouraging students to dig into equity challenges at their schools. Students then develop, in response, an equity-focused project to be implemented throughout the school year. Projects could include conducting peer-to-peer interviews to identify ways schools could assess students' success beyond test scores, developing a play to highlight ways that youth have been agents of change in their community, or hosting an education conference where students dig into their school-level data and recommend strategies for addressing gaps in achievement. Equity projects could be presented to the superintendent or the school board or shared at a student-led education forum hosted in the community.

Family Empowerment

Key to ensuring that families are empowered to lead systemic change as part of an antiracist community is creating the conditions where families feel welcomed, supported, and valued. When these conditions are not in place, the family–school partnership is not cohesive and can, in fact, seem confrontational. School districts frequently underestimate the harm that educational systems have done to the most historically marginalized families and, thus, discount the critical work that is required to earn their trust.

Parents are children's first (and often best) teachers. School staff need to fully understand the hopes and dreams that families have for their children; families, in turn, must work with schools and school districts to make the shifts in practices that will lead to those outcomes. This includes families pushing schools to both offer more rigorous courses and provide the structures and supports that make those courses more accessible.

Collaborating with families. The National PTA and parent–teacher organizations (PTOs) can be very important catalysts for building an antiracist community. Families should work to ensure that these organizations do more than fundraising and hosting dances and similar events—work that truly affects the school's or district's equity challenges. The National PTA (2020) has stated equity goals that have the potential to significantly address disparities in student outcome. Parents who are members of the PTA or PTO should focus on centering the most historically marginalized families in their work, by asking the following questions:

- Do our PTA/PTO leadership and membership represent the diversity of our schools?

- Who is not at the table? Are families of students with disabilities at the table? Families of Indigenous students? Families of students whose home language is not English?

- Are the topics, location, and times of the meetings optimal for engaging these families?

- What conditions need to be created so that historically underrepresented families can be successfully engaged?

At the district level, parents should advocate to be on equity committees to help develop plans, implement strategies, and dig into opportunity gap challenges at their schools. If these committees do not exist, parents should work with the district to establish them. Families could then leverage these committees to advocate for resources to increase equitable outcomes.

Families can also take the lead on developing education compacts or agreements outlining what families can expect from school, what schools can expect from families and students, and how all stakeholders share responsibility for the health and success of their schools. They can conduct interviews with other parents within their same school, across the district, or at other schools outside the district to learn about their experiences and use that information to help create innovative ways that parents can support the success of their schools.

Authentic and equitable family engagement can lead to a stronger sense of belonging at school (Comer & Haynes, 1991; youth.gov, n.d.); improved student outcomes (Fan & Chen, 2001); and the closing of persistent achievement gaps among students of different racial, ethnic, and family income levels (Hatchett, 2015). In this effort, it is critical that families are viewed as co-creators of solutions to challenging equity issues.

Building families' leadership skills. Families must be provided with opportunities to develop their skills and knowledge about how to do this work. Although some families already have these assets and skills, it is important to provide the resources to support them in being able to successfully engage in equity work. Many school districts provide professional development and equity training for school leaders and staff, but they generally do not provide similar knowledge and skill-building opportunities for families. One way that this can be accomplished is through parent academies, like the equity training described for students.

Parent academies can provide an in-depth look at the district's equity priorities, including ways that the curriculum positively reflects the contributions of all peoples and the supports that are available to address gaps in outcomes for specific populations (e.g., students with disabilities, English language learners, other historically marginalized groups). In the absence of organized parent academies, families should reach out to their schools and district to request presentations on equity initiatives. They could also help to design sessions and serve as presenters, increasing the sense of shared ownership for equity work.

Equity-Centered Community Partners

Community partners with culturally specific expertise are essential to working with school districts to address systemic inequity in education. Communities that do this well create various channels for exchanging ideas with community members and engaging them actively in addressing equity gaps.

Increasing representation. Engaging leaders from the Hispanic Chamber of Commerce, a local mosque, the NAACP, the National Urban League, the Anti-Defamation League (ADL), and human rights organizations supports the work of schools by increasing representation across ethnicity, race, and religious differences. School leaders might be used to working with an organization such as ADL or a local mosque to address bullying of students because of religious differences. Expanding this effort to work with organizations that have a specific cultural expertise—such as the local NAACP, to discuss strategies to address the overidentification of boys of color for special education services—helps to create more equal opportunities and outcomes in schools. These organizations have sustained relationships with specific stakeholder groups and thus already have the trust and credibility to engage with them. They also have a deep understanding of the historical content for the equity challenge that exists and knowledge of the actions that the organization and the school district have previously taken to address the challenges. Working in solidarity with organizations with cultural expertise is an essential step to becoming an antiracist community.

Building students' social capital. The community partner—including nonprofits, businesses, faith-based and civic organizations, and the government—can act as an important lever in building social capital for students, including those furthest from opportunities. Social capital includes investment that builds relationships and connections, such as mentoring, internships, externships, and guest speakers. One contributing factor to low engagement at the secondary school level is that often students don't see the connection of what they are learning to their future (Corso et al., 2013). This is especially true for historically marginalized students, who may not have networks of professionals working in careers that require college degrees. This space provides an incredible opportunity for community partners to lean in and address social capital gaps that exist along racial lines. Alumni associations could be a real asset here, too, as could BIPOC students from local colleges and universities, especially historically Black colleges and universities (HBCUs).

Addressing opportunity gaps. Financial investment in schools from community partners can help address opportunity gaps in various ways: by paying for AP testing or field trips, funding professional development to build teacher capacity in implementing culturally affirming pedagogy, sponsoring student awards focused on building scholar identity for underrepresented student groups, and increasing access to co-curricular or extracurricular programs, among others. If a district has some affluent schools that are able to fund art or music teachers due to outside investments from parents and community members, this is a great place for partners committed to an antiracist community to lean in and fund such programs in schools in areas with significantly fewer resources.

The interconnection among employment, housing, health care, and education provides an opportunity for school districts and community partners to align their work to address opportunity gaps. During the COVID-19 pandemic, some school districts partnered with health departments to host COVID vaccination clinics at their schools; providing meals as well made it more convenient for families to access important health and wellness resources. Such partnerships could be expanded to include earlier access to other vaccinations, physicals, wellness check-ups, or employment resources for families. A faith-based partner in the African American community could support the school district by providing an alternative to suspension programs for students focused on helping them develop conflict resolution and restorative practices and connecting students with mentors or student champions in their communities.

Support from Elected Officials

School boards, city or county officials, and state representatives have several key levers that they can use to support a school district in fulfilling the promise of an excellent education for every student. These include establishing laws or policies and creating funding priorities such as capital project investments. The antiracist community holds elected officials accountable for providing the resources to address opportunity gaps. Goals to close gaps in education outcomes should be included in every political platform. Elected officials should be advocating not just for equitable funding for schools, but for adequate funding to support students furthest from opportunity. This includes commitments to obtaining competitive salaries for teachers and ensuring that students have equitable access to high-quality teachers, as well as addressing school zoning to ensure equitable access to high-quality schools. Elected officials who are committed to creating an antiracist community prioritize educational equity in their election platforms and specifically outline their commitments to equity to their constituents.

Community Equity Committees

A community-led equity committee provides a unique opportunity for historically marginalized individuals to have a seat at the table and a voice that influences and informs actions to ensure all students have access to a great education. Creating a racially diverse equity committee drawn from a range of stakeholders—students, families, teachers, administrators, local agencies and organizations, higher education—ensures the community is vested in the school district's equity efforts and is leveraging voices at all levels. The number of members and stakeholder types should be set to ensure equity of voice. For example, it would be important to think of the implications of having a community equity committee where most of the members are school district employees or where the committee does not reflect the diversity of the school and community.

Letting students and their families lead. Students and their families should be the lead voices in a district's equity committee. Too often equity work is *done* to students and their families, instead of *with* them. Other members of the committee should be from partners with a direct connection to the schools—for example, an institution of higher education that focuses on teacher preparation programs or an agency that represents or supports Latinx families.

Although district representatives facilitate the equity committee's conversations and have the responsibility of providing and presenting disaggregated data, the real work of analyzing the root causes of and identifying solutions for the district's opportunity and achievement gaps belongs to the committee. Staff representatives on the district equity committee should include team members from central office departments that support historically marginalized student groups such as migrant students, Native American students, students with disabilities, and English language learners.

Engaging with district leaders. It is important that members of the equity committee see that school and district leaders are actively engaged in their work and that getting to equity is a high priority for the district. District leadership should stay engaged with the equity committee, demonstrating how it is monitoring its equity investments and strategies and reporting on progress toward closing gaps. One way to support this is to ensure that district leadership has frequent opportunities to engage with the equity committee. This could happen by having the committee present to the superintendent on a quarterly basis or having the superintendent attend committee meetings periodically. The purpose of planned engagement is to ensure that the committee provides regular, direct input to district leadership on relevant issues that affect student outcomes.

There are many topics on which equity committees can provide input, from parent involvement to community relations, curriculum adoption and implementation, and cultural competence. Equity committees are invaluable in helping a district define equity or develop an equity policy statement. They can even work with other community partners to create a framework for student–parent contracts that focus on identified achievement and graduation goals or establish a format for hosting community conversations to support increased student and parent engagement.

Digging into challenges. Establishing an equity committee composed of stakeholders from various groups provides an opportunity for districts to create brave spaces for folks to dig into complex issues such as how to address the changing demographics in a school or racially disparate enrollment in gifted and honor programs, plan for new schools or programs, or reallocate resources so that students historically furthest from opportunities have the tools necessary to accelerate growth. Equity committees can play a role in monitoring the district's progress toward closing opportunity gaps. The committee should be expected, and trusted, to review district data disaggregated by race/ethnicity, language proficiency, ability, and any other construct for which disparate outcomes exist.

One way to create the conditions for stakeholders to dig into challenging topics that support the district's equity work is for the group to read a book, an article, or an excerpt together, using the text as an anchor for their work. For example, stakeholders could read and reflect on the following quote from Kathryn M. Neckerman's *Schools Betrayed* (2007):

> Inequality emerged through a myriad of small actions in both the public and private sectors, in domains from politics to work to housing markets to informal social settings. Taken singly, most of these actions appeared reasonable and legally defensible, and sometimes even well-intentioned. Taken together, these actions created a brutally effective system of inequality. The history of [inequity in] schools is a story of damage done by ordinary people taking the path of least resistance. (p. 173)

Addressing inequitable access. The committee—or an offshoot of it— may also focus on issues surrounding equitable access, addressing disparities in quality of and access to rigorous coursework and co-curricular or extracurricular activities. This means spending time examining data such as course enrollment, retention and completion, college admission test scores, and college enrollment and completion, disaggregated by social factors including race, ability, and home language. It is only through a deep dive into data that one can identify disparities, their root causes, and potential solutions. The committee could host community conversations about gaps in education outcomes and center the voices of historically marginalized groups. In many high schools in America, students of color are grossly underrepresented in the rigorous courses that are gatekeepers for college admission and scholarships (Center for American Progress, 2021).

Although joining a school district equity committee or task force is an important strategy, sometimes community members lead this charge by establishing equity groups themselves. One example of this is a community equity team composed of leaders from community-based advocacy organizations working to eliminate the ethnic or racial predictability of students' achievement and closing opportunity gaps. In this example, the school district supports the community equity leadership team by attending their monthly meeting to provide district insight, input, and data to support the topics being discussed.

It is important for the district to open its doors to the community. However, the district should also seek opportunities to participate in equity work in the community space. District staff can serve on community advisory boards, including a local (city or county) human relations board or community committees focused on addressing disproportionate minority contact with judicial systems.

 # Roadblocks

Engaging in true, transformative antiracist work that will lead to the closing of racialized gaps in opportunity and achievement takes the whole community. You can expect to encounter roadblocks such as a resistance to power sharing and the politicization of and opposition to equity work.

Resistance to Power Sharing

Community engagement work can be hard, and it doesn't always land on the solutions that education leaders believe are ideal. Sharing power is a leadership skill that enhances community engagement. However, it is imperative that school and district leaders do this work *with* students and their families, rather than *for* them. You've probably heard the African adage "If you want to go fast, go alone. But if you want to go far, go with others." This is especially true if you want to establish an antiracist community.

Opposition to Equity Work

Across the country, those involved in educational equity work face challenges. School boards have become more partisan. Board members who would like to lean into bold and courageous actions to support closing racialized gaps in achievement are finding themselves called extremist and, in some cases, anti-American. In 2023, over 30 bills were introduced in state legislatures targeting diversity, equity, and inclusion efforts (Lieb, 2023). Opposition to critical race theory (see Chapter 5), an academic and legal framework that describes systemic racism in American society, alleges that viewing society and history through this lens is intended to make White students feel bad about or responsible for the country's racist history.

This is a major roadblock, and many school and district leaders as a result lack the political will to do the work required to reach equity in education. To get around this roadblock, the community needs to intentionally build relationships with elected leaders. As discussed earlier in this chapter, ensure that your elected leaders have a clear and deep understanding of the equity challenges (based on data) and of strategies that the district is currently using and those that are part of its future strategic plan. Provide small-group engagements just for elected officials to provide updates and overviews and to give them space to ask questions on the district's equity work. Invite elected officials to youth-led and family-led forums so they can hear from their con-stituents about the value and effects of the equity work. Become aware of elected officials' priorities, and lean into connecting those commitments with the work that is most essential to get to educational equity.

 ## Shortcuts

Engaging antiracist community leaders across all sectors and aligning the work of each are essential to reaching sustained equity transformation. Despite the roadblocks, some shortcuts can be used to accelerate progress toward creating an antiracist school district.

Assess Your Assets

What are the strengths in your community, as well as in each stakeholder group? Develop an asset map, identifying student and parent groups, commu-nity organizations, and equity-centered organizations. Before you create new equity workstreams or structures, assess what is already in place to address educational equity. Where it makes sense, connect to your district's work and build upon existing structures (e.g., PTAs/PTOs, NAACP or other groups supporting historically marginalized groups).

Start the Conversation

Invite stakeholders to come together to start a conversation about creating an antiracist community to address educational equity. In your conversations, center the needs of students in historically marginalized groups and students who are not thriving in school. Ensure that your conversations lean into the assets that each group brings to the table and the important role that *they* will play in determining what they need. Provide space to hear from students and their families regarding their educational experiences. Create opportunities for diverse representatives from every stakeholder group to have a seat at the equity table and an equal voice in the conversation.

 Rest Stop

At this rest stop, we challenge you to reflect on the following questions surrounding community engagement and alignment:

- How can the community work in solidarity with the school district to address racialized gaps in student outcomes?

- What opportunities are provided for students and families to be co-creators of solutions for the most challenging equity issues?

- What organizations are already leaning into equity? How can there be stronger alignment and connection between their work and the school district's equity priorities?

CONCLUSION:
LEADING SYSTEMIC CHANGE

*Equity isn't handing a kid a laptop. It's knowing
the systemic conditions that led to the lack of
the laptop and working to mitigate them.*

—Ericka Garcia, *Edutopia*

Getting to equity in education is a journey, not a destination. This work is an ongoing process in an ever-changing world and political landscape. Throughout this book, we have focused on ways that various stakeholders can further educational equity. However, the strategic, collaborative, and coordinated actions of school districts is critical to real, sustained transformation. It is time now to pull together the understandings from the preceding chapters to further systemic, antiracist work in education.

All journeys begin with a first step. The journey toward racial equity in education includes establishing the "why," reviewing and interrogating data, establishing a leadership team, and identifying expected outcomes (e.g., key performance indicators). Once you've started, the next step is to keep going. Sounds obvious, right? But staying the course is easier said than done in our politically polarized world. Finally, this work requires leaders, advocates, allies, and co-conspirators who are able and willing to create sustainable change that leads to embedding equity and antiracist practices into the culture of the school district and the community.

Conduct an Equity Audit

Regardless of where an individual, a school, a district, or a community is on the antiracist journey, the first step is to assess the current situation compared to the goal. You must begin with knowing where you are and where you are going, to avoid wasting valuable resources (including time). Conducting a systemic equity audit and SWOT (strengths, weaknesses, opportunities, and threats) analysis can help direct attention to root causes of equity gaps. In the Introduction, we discussed how to audit aspects of the education system for equity. In Chapters 1 through 6, we provided benchmarks for contributors to the education system: the curriculum, the teachers, the school leaders, the central office staff, the district leaders, and the community. Review the Roadblocks and Shortcuts for each stakeholder group, and identify primary takeaways that will support the initial work of establishing an antiracist school district. Getting started requires establishing a commitment to equity and antiracism. Initial steps include establishing the *why* and a review and interrogation of data, establishing a leadership team, and identifying expected outcomes to include key performance indicators. Teachers; school and central office staff, parents, and students; and community stakeholders should be a part of the conversations from the onset of the journey. Each should be clear about their roles in the success of the journey. Each should contribute by identifying champions and allies who will support the work. Finally, each should also be aware of accountability measures that will help drive the work forward.

Develop an Action Plan

You are familiar with the various aspects of strategic planning, including mission and vision statements and school improvement or community action plans identifying long- and short-term SMARTIE goals (see Chapter 4). SMARTIE goals—which are designed to be *s*trategic, *m*easurable, *a*mbitious, *r*ealistic, *t*ime-bound, *i*nclusive, and *e*quitable—demand an intentional focus on improving outcomes for students who are Black, Indigenous, or people of color. On the journey to equity in education, planning includes identifying human and fiscal needs and resources (within the school, district, and community), as well as identifying benchmarks or developing a "balanced scorecard" describing objectives that can be measured, to monitor progress.

After identifying your goals, it is critical to outline the action steps necessary to reach each goal. This includes identifying key stakeholders, whose engagement is essential, along with the required resources.

Getting to equity is an adaptive challenge—the problems may be unknown or unspoken, hard to identify and tied to deeper patterns. This means that in addition to identifying technical solutions such as resources (people, money, time), training, and policies, you will need to identify adaptive solutions to change mindsets and individual behaviors. Throughout this book, we have offered recommendations, practices, and approaches that can be implemented in all areas of the education system; many of these (see the Shortcuts) can be leveraged for quick wins. We encourage you to review the reflection questions at the end of the chapters when you begin this work.

Implement the Plan

Once started, continuing the journey toward equity and antiracism means understanding and following through with a strategic planning implementation process and monitoring progress along the journey. Superintendents must set an equity vision and ensure that this work is clearly articulated in the district strategic plan (see Chapter 5). Although often led by the superintendent, district leaders, and board of education, success is more likely when this is a collaborative endeavor. Although more school districts are establishing chief equity officers or directors of diversity, equity, and inclusion (DEI), it is common in smaller districts for the superintendent to lead equity work. Being intentional and consistent is necessary to keep going while establishing a team of equity champions who are invested in improving outcomes for all children but particularly those who have experienced limited success in school.

Setting and stating clear goals, identifying risks, assigning tasks, and allocating necessary resources are critical steps in strategic plan implementation. The plan should also define scheduled checkpoints for monitoring progress and include regular updates based on need and determined by a rubric or the balanced scorecard. Using a strategic planning tool that includes a balanced scorecard or online tools can help with this process. One might also consider using a project plan template that will identify the person responsible for each task along with clearly defined timelines and detailed status monitoring information. This is a flexible document that could be updated routinely to guide the process.

Monitor Progress

Progress monitoring and frequent updates (at least quarterly) are essential to ensuring that the journey is moving in the right direction. Monitoring is a way to identify successes and celebrate wins along the way, and it ranges from the use of simple checklists (not the most informative) to mini-audits of the work. Without monitoring, all you have is POTS: a plan on the shelf. A POTS may be a remarkable plan, on paper, but without progress monitoring, it will not support the journey toward educational equity and antiracism.

Focus on Equity

As the strategic plan is implemented and monitored, paying close attention to the specific equity and antiracist efforts is necessary to keep going. The most successful districts are intentional about creating specific organizational structures that lend themselves to embarking in the work and monitoring it. A district reorganization is not required for this. When the budget allows, establishing an equity officer or a department that prioritizes DEI and belonging is ideal.

With the rise of opposition to and fear of critical race theory, some districts have shifted away from identifying a staff member as chief equity officer or director of DEI. Regardless of the title, someone must own and be responsible for leading the development and implementation of an equity policy and leading equity leadership teams and task forces. The person in this role should also lead, plan, and conduct data meetings; ensure the allocation of resources and research; and support professional learning for teachers, leaders, and staff.

Course Correct as Needed

Progress monitoring will reveal whether a course correction is needed. During routine monitoring, the following should be considered to determine whether the journey is on track:

- Which goals are on track and which are not?
- Have adequate funds been allocated for successful implementation?
- Do key performance indicators support improving outcomes?
- Are the right people in place to lead and support plan implementation?

Ideally, the answer to each of these questions is yes. One "no" response demonstrates a need to revisit that area and address shortcomings. The team lead should decide the next steps. Two or more "no" responses indicate a need for course correction. In this case, take time to review all relevant data; assess root causes; and adjust the timeline, budget, key performance indicators, and team members to enhance the opportunity for success. There is no shame in having to make a course correction. In fact, it is wise to do so early in the journey to increase the likelihood of success.

Celebrate Wins

As we've said repeatedly, this work is complex, multifaceted, political, and hard. Because there is the potential for team members to become weary or suffer from burnout, it is important to take time to celebrate even the smallest wins and to practice wellness and self-care. Leaders should be intentional about identifying and rewarding exemplars across stakeholders within the district. On-the-spot notes of praise along with a gift card or other token of gratitude and shout-outs during team meetings are simple ways to show stakeholders that their work is valued. It is also important to determine how to formally celebrate the equity work, either as part of other celebrations or in an annual "Closing the Gap" awards banquet or similar special event.

Wellness and self-care time must be deliberate in order to keep going. If wellness teams are in place, they can lead this charge. Employees should have access to an employee assistance program, regular wellness tips, and time and space to practice self-care. This is most effective when modeled by leaders and done out of genuine commitment rather than as a job obligation. And remember to be kind to yourself and others. Be generous with grace.

Sustaining Change Systemwide

Getting to equity demands cultural shifts and instituting structures that enable sustainability. Being collaborative and transparent with employees and other stakeholders makes this possible. Effective personnel planning will help ensure that there are owners of the work as the journey evolves. As school districts move through this journey, leaders should empower all teachers, leaders, and staff to lead from their current seat.

Collaboration and Transparency

"Collaboration and transparency" means routinely sharing decision-making power and voice, as well as establishing mechanisms to share equity updates, including web pages, social media posts, and videos. Opportunities for two-way communication and feedback, such as town hall meetings, equity task-force updates, and chats with leadership are important. Collaboration and transparency give school district staff and the community a bird's-eye view of the equity and antiracism journey. Doing this well allows the school district to build advocacy, which may minimize pushback as the journey continues and prevent disruptions that could potentially stall (or stop) the work.

Building Internal and External Capacity

With a national teacher shortage, it is more important than ever for school districts to focus on talent development. To effectively sustain an equity and antiracism plan requires hiring effectively while also building a leadership pipeline. Hiring talent who are aligned with district core values and who have a heart and desire to embark in equity work is the best practice. Doing so allows schools and districts to move faster and to go deeper while building sustainable practices.

Building an internal leadership pipeline (see Chapters 4 and 5) supports sustainability efforts by creating and empowering current and future leaders with the tools, resources, and knowledge needed to lean into and lead equity work effectively. As efforts are sustained, expectations are more likely to become embedded into the school and district culture. Districts should provide sustained professional development, coaching, and support to the central office and school-based staff who are leading the work, and provide support staff at varying levels of proficiency with appropriate training experiences.

Some Parting Advice

Being a champion for educational equity and antiracism requires courage, but you are not in this alone. Although your journey may start as a lonely one, courageous equity champions are out there, waiting to connect with you and get onboard.

Teachers, school and central office leaders, superintendents, students, parents, and community stakeholders all can and must be a part of the conversation, and each has a role to play in the success of the journey. Each group includes potential champions and allies. And because most public school districts across the United States are now monitoring gaps by race and see those demographic gap-closing metrics in their state accountability systems, now is the perfect time to lean on a plan for educational equity.

Ultimately, it will take an incredible amount of strategic alignment, momentum, and transformation to turn the tide of centuries of racism and racist practices that continue to impact the achievement of BIPOC students. As long as student academic, behavioral, and cultural outcomes continue to be predicated on race, ethnicity, language, gender, sexual orientation, and socioeconomic level, there will still be equity work to do.

For the United States to truly live out its foundational principles of equality for all, we must get to educational equity. Ensuring that all students feel a strong sense of belonging in their school, have access to rigorous and culturally responsive curriculum and instruction, and have the support of school staff who care deeply for them and nurture their identities as scholars are all key to reaching this destination. We are certainly not yet where we want and need to be. The underdevelopment of the talents and potential of children of color, particularly Black children, continues to be among the nation's greatest moral and economic failures. We must do better; our children and our future are counting on us. Stay the course. The journey will be worthwhile.

APPENDIX:
CASE STUDIES

Every school district's journey to educational equity is unique. Having presented the journey from perspectives of the key stakeholders, in this appendix, we offer for consideration the intersections of various challenges and how different stakeholders might work together in tandem to move their district toward its racial equity goals. The following are examples of what the journey toward educational equity might look like in three fictional districts that have different assets and are facing different sets of risks.

Case Study 1: Acorn School District

A Community Rallying Cry

Although the central office and school-based staff in Acorn School District would say they are nonracist, most believe that the district lacks awareness of how its practices fail to meet the needs of students of color and their families. There is a significant gap in achievement when data from statewide assessments are disaggregated by race, with students who are BIPOC scoring more than 20 percent below their White peers. School leaders in Acorn have had limited training to support their development of culturally responsive instruction or strategies to address equity gaps. The district has few people of color in leadership positions, and the previous superintendent did not prioritize closing equity gaps.

The district uses the state-adopted curriculum, which includes some resources centering the experiences and contributions of BIPOC. However, most of the time, students who are BIPOC do not see people who look like them or from similar backgrounds reflected in their learning. Teachers commonly report "not seeing color," but students who are BIPOC are apprehensive about speaking up during class discussions; many families believe that teachers display sympathy rather than empathy to children in poverty. Although students who are BIPOC represent 40 percent of the district's enrollment, honors, gifted education, and Advanced Placement (AP) classes are overwhelmingly White. In addition, White students' participation in extracurricular activities is more than twice that of students of color.

A few years ago, the entire community became concerned about the academic underperformance of students of color, as well as the overrepresentation of these same students in suspensions and special-education identification. The school board met these challenges head-on and joined arms with the community to implement change. Two years ago, a new superintendent was hired and given the charge of addressing these persistent equity gaps. After conducting a year-long "listening and learning" tour, she is ready to lead the district on its equity journey and has identified her first steps.

Step 1: Engage the community. The genesis of the school district's move to address its educational equity gaps was community concern regarding disparate racial outcomes. The superintendent recognizes the need to keep the community informed and engaged—and that means giving them a variety of opportunities to provide input on strategies to address the equity concerns that they rallied to address. Another strategy that she is considering is forming a community-led equity task force; this group could provide a way for the school district to have greater accountability to its stakeholders and also give the community greater buy-in to the success of the educational equity work.

Step 2: Improve curriculum resources and professional development. The state's curriculum resources are starting to be more inclusive (i.e., include more racially and culturally diverse content), and this is an asset that the superintendent should maximize. Any time there is a new curriculum or new curriculum resources, it is important to provide training for teachers and exemplars of how to best implement these resources.

Culturally responsive instruction can increase student engagement in learning—and this is a practice that teachers in the district have struggled with. In addition to professional development in this area, the superintendent and school leaders should increase teacher voice and choice in assignments to support student engagement and inclusivity. Acorn SD also has not previously provided professional development to support principals to lead equity work. Building the capacity of school leaders is critical to the success of any school transformation strategy. Strengthening principals' skills in being able to support culturally responsive instruction is key to sustaining the work long term.

Step 3: Increase access to enrichment. The underrepresentation of students of color in rigorous coursework (e.g., AP, gifted education) is another important area for the district to address. The superintendent is planning to bring together representatives from various schools and stakeholder groups to dig into the data on AP and gifted education enrollment by race and by school. This process will help them identify the root cause of its racially disparate outcomes. She also plans to hold focus group meetings with students to understand the barriers they face to enrolling in these higher-level courses.

Step 4: Develop an equity policy. Because the school board is open to collaborating with members of the community to implement change, the superintendent recognizes that this is the time to develop an equity policy for approval by the board. Such a policy would solidify the board's vision for educational equity and its commitment to providing resources to address opportunity gaps. It would also establish how the district will measure and monitor its process toward eliminating inequities.

Case Study 2: Beacon School System

Addressing Community Backlash to Equity Work

Beacon School System is a school district that many believe is already prioritizing equity. It established an equity policy five years ago and has spent time expanding its view of diversity to include other socially oppressed groups, including its growing population of English learners and new immigrant families. At both the school and district levels, staff carry out intentionally inclusive efforts including recruiting BIPOC and ensuring that historically marginalized voices have access to both informal and formal leadership roles. The current curriculum and resources recognize the racial diversity of the student body and acknowledge the contributions of BIPOC. Teachers are trained in trauma-informed and culturally responsive teaching practices. Many teachers differentiate instruction to meet the needs of the individual students in their classrooms. On a recent statewide climate survey, Beacon exceeded the state average regarding the percentage of BIPOC students who indicated that teachers developed not only good relationships but deep relationships with their students. Schools provide antibias training for teachers and staff, and school leaders frame all goals in their improvement plans through an equity lens.

However, there is a growing cloud of concern regarding further equity work in Beacon. The recent national debates and protests regarding critical race theory and "Don't Say Gay" legislation have taken a toll. Some student-led rallies in support of Black Lives Matter were met with strong and almost violent opposition. Several board members recently lost their seats to individuals who campaigned on the premise that the district efforts were radical and hurt White children.

The superintendent is in the fourth year of his initial contract; his contract was renewed for another four years just before the last board election. He and many central office leaders are worried about next steps on their journey to educational equity in view of changes in the school board. However, school leaders—and, more important, the strong teachers' union—are adamant that the district is on the right path. The teachers' union's equity committee has been strategizing on how to avoid losing the progress the district has made on its journey and ways the stakeholders in Beacon might move forward on their equity journey.

Step 1: Build relationships. This superintendent's first step is to spend some time building relationships with the new school board members individually—and with the board as a whole. The superintendent is in a good position, having had his contract renewed, but the divisions within the board create a potentially volatile situation. He recognizes that the new board members ran on a platform in opposition to the equity agenda; what is the vision for the board holistically? He needs to learn who the new board members are, what they value and believe, and what their education priorities are.

Step 2: Share successes and perspectives. The superintendent has a key role in sharing the district's work. Often, individuals who are not physically in school classrooms have blind spots and misconceptions surrounding what they think is happening there. The superintendent needs to build the new board members' knowledge and awareness of the district's efforts to improve education outcomes for all students—leading with data.

Getting key stakeholders in front of the board provides on-the-ground perspectives of the equity challenges and the current path that the district is on. One key stakeholder group is teachers; because the teachers' union in Beacon is a strong advocate of the equity work, their support should be maximized. Teachers, and especially teachers' unions, can be very powerful tools for initiating education reform. The union representatives need to be able to clearly communicate and demonstrate how the district's equity strategies are helping to improve learning conditions for all students. Student and parent voices are important levers to lean into if the district wants to ensure that its equity work continues. The district should set up student focus groups, parent focus groups, and/or parent and student focus groups. School board members need to see what the work looks like in classrooms, to hear personal stories, and to see examples of the work. The superintendent's challenge is to demystify "culturally responsive instruction" and other terms that the new board members perceive to be divisive and detrimental to White students.

Case Study 3: Cleverton Public Schools

Building Teacher Capacity

In the Cleverton Public Schools district, most of the students are BIPOC, but the majority of the teachers and school leaders are not. The district leadership has a growing understanding of systemic racism and has held training for all staff. The district identifies as an "antiracist" institution, and the school board policy aligns to this vision. One of the district's priorities is actively recruiting and promoting BIPOC and other groups historically denied access and opportunities. In the past three years, the number of BIPOC in leadership positions has more than doubled, growing from 10 to 22. However, in this large school district, these individuals represent only 5 percent of the leaders.

The district has engaged in an equity audit of its curriculum and is working with a consultant to create supplemental materials that center the experiences of historically marginalized peoples. Although some teachers are already creating brave spaces for students, teaching from a whole-child perspective, and personalizing instruction, this does not change the fact that most teachers in the district are White and many struggle to develop relationships with their students. Teachers at the secondary level are concerned about district implementation of policies that limit the use of suspension and worried that opening their honors and AP classrooms to "nontraditional" students will reduce the course's "rigor." Some teachers have begun to express those concerns to families, and it is creating some community challenges for school leaders who were originally in support of these shifts.

Community stakeholders are engaged in learning about systemic racism and its effect on education and other systems, including housing, health care, and finance. A few equity-focused nonprofit organizations are actively working to support the district's equity vision. However, the community is about evenly split between those who support the district's equity work and those who think it is being done to the detriment of White students in the district.

Step 1: Engage early adopters. Cleverton has many things already in place to support a successful equity journey, and it already has bright spots and exemplars on which to build. The superintendent understands that teachers are key to significant school-level (and thus district-level) change and is planning professional development to build teacher competencies in culturally responsive practices that support students from diverse backgrounds. Teachers who are already using a whole child approach and creating brave spaces can provide examples and models as part of this professional development work and also co-present or co-design the training. These early adopters also can be tapped to lead professional learning communities that provide support throughout the school year and sustain teaching expertise.

Step 2: Improve disciplinary practices. The superintendent needs to spend time with secondary principals to clarify why decreasing the use of out-of-school suspensions as a disciplinary measure is necessary, leading with research regarding how implicit bias contributes to disparate discipline consequences. Reflecting national rates, in Cleverton, students who are BIPOC are more likely to receive suspensions than their White peers, even for the same offenses. District- and school-level teams need to spend time getting to the root causes of disparate suspension data and engage students in the conversation of what is needed to support positive behavior. Student focus groups will help school teams gain greater perspective on the challenges they face, including feeling "policed." The superintendent's plan is to implement additional supports—mental health services, teacher training, positive incentive programs, restorative and trauma-responsive practices—in tandem with the reduced use of suspension.

Step 3: Increase access to rigorous courses. Teachers who express concern about opening the most rigorous coursework to "nontraditional" students are indirectly acknowledging who has historically had access to such courses—and highlighting the need to address teacher bias about the academic abilities of students who are BIPOC. What is behind their beliefs and mindsets? Is it possible that students of color are less likely to get into advanced courses than their White peers, even if they have higher grades? Tools like teacher recommendations serve as biased gatekeepers of and barriers to advanced learning opportunities. Again, focus groups would allow teachers to hear directly from students of color regarding their experiences in advanced courses and help school leaders identify strategies to create a pipeline to AP and honors courses for students of color.

The pipeline to rigorous coursework in secondary school begins in elementary school; academic gaps start early and become more exacerbated over time. The district leaders need to do a deep dive into assessing the rigor of *all* courses. For example, are courses labeled as "college prep" really ensuring that students are ready for postsecondary work? Do students in every grade have access to grade-level-appropriate assignments?

Step 4: Strengthen community partnerships. The district needs to strengthen its relationships with equity-focused nonprofits and to deeply understand how the efforts of these organizations are moving the needle toward its own equity goals. These equity-focused partners can support the district's equity work by providing training and information sessions for the broader community. These trainings, in turn, will help the community to learn more about the district's equity work, which can address concerns fueled by misinformation or lack of information. Strengthening community partnerships will also help the district to identify those who can help address gaps and support students, their families, and school staff.

REFERENCES

Alvarez, B. (2021, May 27). We need to teach the truth about systemic racism, say educators. *NEA News*. https://www.nea.org/advocating-for-change/new-from-nea/we-need-teach-truth-about-systemic-racism-say-educators

American Civil Liberties Union. (2023). *Cops and no counselors. How the lack of school mental health staff is harming students*. https://www.aclu.org/issues/juvenile-justice/school-prison-pipeline/cops-and-no-counselors

American University. (n.d.). *The antiracist curriculum development initiative in the College of Arts and Sciences*. https://www.american.edu/cas/about/upload/antiracist-curriculum-dev.pdf

America's Promise Alliance, Aspen Education & Society Program, & Council of Chief State School Officers. (2018). *States leading for equity: Promising practices advancing the equity commitments*. https://www.ccsso.org/sites/default/files/2018-02/States%20Leading%20for%20Equity%20Online.pdf

AtRisk Youth Programs. (2023). *Different federal grant programs to help at risk youths*. https://atriskyouthprograms.com/different-federal-grant-programs-to-help-at-risk-youths/

Boschma, J., & Brownstein, R. (2016, February 29). The concentration of poverty in American schools. *The Atlantic*. https://www.theatlantic.com/education/archive/2016/02/concentration-poverty-american-schools/471414/

Brown, B. (2012). *Daring greatly: How the courage to be vulnerable transforms the way we live, love, parent and lead*. Penguin.

Burke, L. M., & Schwalbach, J. (2021, March 11). *Housing redlining and its lingering effects on education opportunity*. Heritage Foundation. https://www.heritage.org/sites/default/files/2021-03/BG3594.pdf

Burnham, K. (2020, July 31). *5 Culturally responsive teaching strategies*. Northeastern University. https://www.northeastern.edu/graduate/blog/culturally-responsive-teaching-strategies/

Carrillo, S., & Salhotra, P. (2022, July 14). *The U.S. student population is more diverse, but schools are still highly segregated.* NPR. https://www.npr.org/2022/07/14/1111060299/school-segregation-report

Center for American Progress. (2021, June 30). *Closing advanced coursework equity gaps for all students.* https://www.americanprogress.org/article/closing-advanced-coursework-equity-gaps-students/

Center on Education Policy. (2007, June). *Answering the question that matters most: Has student achievement increased since No Child Left Behind?* https://files.eric.ed.gov/fulltext/ED520272.pdf

Chambers, T. V. (2009). The "receivement gap": School tracking policies and the fallacy of the "achievement gap." *Journal of Negro Education, 78*(4), 417–431. https://www.jstor.org/stable/25676096

Chen, G. (2023, March 10). *Students of color disproportionately disciplined in schools.* Public School Review. https://www.publicschoolreview.com/blog/students-of-color-disproportionately-disciplined-in-schools

Coleman, J. S., Campbell, E. Q., Hobson, C. J., McPartland, J., Mood, A. M., Weinfeld, F. D., & York, R. L. (1966). *Equality of educational opportunity* (ED012275). https://files.eric.ed.gov/fulltext/ED012275.pdf

Comer, J. P., & Haynes, N. M. (1991, January). Parent involvement in schools: An ecological approach. *Elementary School Journal, 91*(3), 271–277. https://www.jstor.org/stable/1001713

Connors, N. A. (2000). *If you don't feed the teachers, they eat the students! Guide to success for administrators and teachers.* Incentive Publications.

Corso, M. J., Bundick, M. J., Quaglia, R. J., & Haywood, D. E. (2013). *American Secondary Education, 41*(3), 50–61. https://www.jstor.org/stable/43694167

Council of Chief State School Officers. (2019, January). *A vision and guidance for a diverse and learner-ready teacher workforce.* https://ccsso.org/sites/default/files/2019-01/Vision%20and%20Guidance%20for%20a%20Diverse%20and%20Learner-Ready%20Teacher%20Workforce_FINAL010919.pdf

Darling-Hammond, L. (1998, March 1). *Unequal opportunity: Race and education.* Brookings. https://www.brookings.edu/articles/unequal-opportunity-race-and-education/

De Brey, C., Misu, L., McFarland, J., Wilkinson-Flicker, Diliberti, M., Zhang, A., Branstetter, C., & Wang, X. (2019, February). *Status and trends in the education of racial and ethnic groups 2018* (NCES 219-038). National Center for Education Statistics, Institute for Education Statistics. https://nces.ed.gov/pubs2019/2019038.pdf

Delpit, L. (2013). *Multiplication is for White people: Raising expectations for other people's children.* New Press.

Desimone, L. M., & Long, D. (2010). Teacher effects and the achievement gap: Do teacher and teaching quality influence the achievement gap between Black and

White and high- and low-SES students in the early grades? *Teachers College Record, 112*(12), 3024–3073. https://doi.org/10.1177/016146811011201206

Desmond-Harris, J. (2017, January 5). The myth about smart black kids and "acting white" that won't die. *Vox*. https://www.vox.com/identities/2017/1/5/14175116/acting-white-myth-black-kids-academics-school-achievement-gap-debunked

edbuild.org. (n.d.). *Nonwhite school districts get $23 billion less than white districts*. https://edbuild.org/content/23-billion

EdPost. (2021, August 12). *Explained: What is Title I and how is it used to fund our schools?* https://www.edpost.com/explainer/explained-what-is-title-i-and-how-is-it-used-to-fund-our-schools

Education Trust. (2020, January 9). *Black and Latino students shut out of advanced coursework opportunities*. https://edtrust.org/press-release/black-and-latino-students-shut-out-of-advanced-coursework-opportunities/

El-Mekki, S. (2021, September 9). *To achieve educational justice, we need more Black teachers*. EdSurge. https://www.edsurge.com/news/2021-09-09-to-achieve-educational-justice-we-need-more-black-teachers

The Equity and Excellence Commission. (2013). *For each and every child—A strategy for education equity and excellence*. U.S. Department of Education. https://oese.ed.gov/files/2020/10/equity-excellence-commission-report.pdf

EveryStudentSucceedsAct.org. (n.d.). *Every Student Succeeds Act (ESSA): A comprehensive guide*. https://www.everystudentsucceedsact.org

Fan, X., & Chen, M. (2001). Parental involvement and students' academic achievement: A meta-analysis. *Educational Psychology Review, 13*(1), 1–22. https://doi.org/10.1023/A:1009048817385

Farrington, C. (2019). *Equitable learning and development: Applying science to foster liberatory education*. Applied Developmental Science. https://doi.org/10.1080/10888691.2019.1609730

Fisher, D., Frey, N., & Hattie, J. A. (2016). *Visible learning for literacy*. Corwin.

Fullan, M. (2007). *The new meaning of educational change*. Teachers College Press.

Gamoran, A. (2009, August). *Tracking and inequality: New directions for research and practice*. Wisconsin Center for Education Research. https://eric.ed.gov/?id=ED506617

Garcia, A., DeRamus-Byers, R., & Silva, E., Brosnan, J., Duffet, A., Dunn, R., Entrekin, K., McLean Kesler, C., Manuel, A., Greenberg Motamedi, J., & Pasterkiewicz, R. (2022, September 29). *Grow your own educators: A toolkit for program design and development*. New America. https://www.newamerica.org/education-policy/reports/grow-your-own-toolkit/#authors

García, E., & Weiss, E. (2017, September 27). *Reducing and averting achievement gaps*. Economic Policy Institute. https://www.epi.org/publication/reducing-and-averting-achievement-gaps/

Garrett, N. C. (2012). *A study of the perceptions of school system personnel of the academic achievement gap and how their perceptions influence their educational practices* [Unpublished doctoral dissertation, North Carolina State University]. https://repository.lib.ncsu.edu/handle/1840.16/7913

Gay, G. (2000). *Culturally responsive teaching: Theory, research, and practice.* Teachers College Press.

Gay, G. (2002, March–April). Preparing for culturally responsive teaching. *Journal of Teacher Education, 53*(2), 106–116.

Gershenson, S., Hart, C. M. D., Hyman, J., Lindsay, C., & Papageorge, N. W. (2022). The long-run impacts of same-race teachers. *American Economic Journal: Economic Policy, 14*(4), 300–342. https://doi.org/10.1257/pol.20190573

Ghandnoosh, N., & Nellis, A. (2022, September 8). *How many people are spending over a decade in prison?* The Sentencing Project. https://www.sentencingproject .org/policy-brief/how-many-people-are-spending-over-a-decade-in-prison/

Glover, J., & Miguel, K. (2020, July 9). *What are structural, institutional and systemic racism?* ABC News. https://abc7news.com/systemic-racism-definition -structural-institutionalized-what-is/6292530/

Gonen, Y. (2015, June 13). Black students are more likely to get "ineffective" teachers: Report. *New York Post.* https://nypost.com/2015/06/13/black-students-are-more -likely-to-get-ineffective-teachers-report/

Gonzalez, S. B., Morton, M., Patel, S., & Samuels, B. (2021). *Youth of color disproportionately impacted by housing instability.* Chapin Hall at the University of Chicago. https://www.chapinhall.org/research/youth -of-color-disproportionately-impacted-by-housing-instability/#:~:text= The%20risks%20of%20homelessness%20and,re%2Dentering%20 homelessness%20after%20exiting.

Gross, T. (2022, February 3). From slavery to socialism, new legislation restricts what teachers can discuss. *Fresh Air.* https://www.npr.org/2022/02/03/ 1077878538/legislation-restricts-what-teachers-can-discuss

Hammond, Z. (2014). *Culturally responsive teaching and the brain.* Corwin.

Hanover Research. (2017, February). *School-based strategies for narrowing the achievement gap.* https://www.wasa-oly.org/WASA/images/WASA/1.0%20 Who%20We%20Are/1.4.1.6%20SIRS/Download_Files/LI%202017/May-%20 School-Based%20Strategies%20for%20Narrowing%20the%20Achievement %20Gap.pdf

Hanushek, E. A., Peterson, P. E., Talpey, L. M., & Woessmann, L. (2019). The achievement gap fails to close. *EducationNext, 19*(3).

Harris, J. (2020, January 16). *What is MTSS?* Renaissance. https://www.renaissance .com/2020/01/16/blog-what-is-mtss-how-to-explain-mtss-to-almost-anyone/

Hatchett, D. (2015). *Closing the achievement gap: The critical importance of parental engagement.* Oxford Education blog. https://educationblog.oup.com/primary/ closing-the-achievement-gap-the-critical-importance-of-parental-engagement

Hattie, J. (2015). *Visible learning in action.* Taylor & Francis. https://doi.org/10.4324/ 9781315722603

Houston, D. M., Peterson, P. E., & West, M. R. (2022). Partisan rifts widen, perceptions of school quality decline. *Education Next, 23*(1). https://www.education next.org/partisan-rifts-widen-perceptions-school-quality-decline-results-2022 -education-next-survey-public-opinion/

Howard County Public Schools. (2020). *Policy 1080—Educational equity.* https:// policy.hcpss.org/1000/1080/

Jean, M. (2016). Can you "work your way up?" Ability grouping and the development of academic engagement [Unpublished doctoral dissertation]. University of Chicago. https://knowledge.uchicago.edu/record/577

Kellogg Insight. (2018, October 2). *How peer pressure can lead teens to underachieve—Even in schools where it's "cool to be smart."* https://insight.kellogg .northwestern.edu/article/peer-pressure-can-lead-teens-underachieve -schools-cool-to-be-smart

Kendi, I. X. (2019). *How to be an antiracist.* One World.

Ladson-Billings, G. (2006). From the achievement gap to the education debt: Understanding achievement in U.S. schools. *Educational Researcher, 35*(7), 3–12. https://doi.org/10.3102/0013189X035007003

Learning Policy Institute. (2023). *Whole child education.* https://learningpolicy institute.org/topic/whole-child-education

Lee, J. (2004). Multiple facets of inequity in racial and ethnic achievement gaps. *Peabody Journal of Education, 79*(2), 51–73. https://doi.org/10.1207/ s15327930pje7902_5

Lee, J., & Wong, K. W. (2004). The impact of accountability on racial and socioeconomic equity: Considering both school resources and achievement outcomes. *American Educational Research Journal, 41*(4), 797–832. https://doi.org/ 10.3102/00028312041004797

Lieb, D. A. (2023, April 17). GOP states targeting diversity, equity efforts in higher ed. *AP.* https://apnews.com/article/diversity-equity-inclusion-legislation -7bd8d4d52aaaa9902dde59a257874686

Lleras, C., & Rangel, C. (2009). Ability grouping practices in elementary school and African American/Hispanic achievement. *American Journal of Education, 115*(2), 279–304.

Lozenski, B. D. (2017). Beyond mediocrity: The dialectics of crisis in the continuing miseducation of Black youth. *Harvard Educational Review, 87*(2), 161–185. https://doi.org/10.17763/1943-5045-87.2.161

McGirt, E. (2020, June 1). Citigroup, Netflix, and Microsoft among companies making statements in support of Black lives and justice. *Fortune.* https://fortune .com/2020/06/01/citigroup-netflix-microsoft-racism-george-floyd-police -brutality-statements-business/

Mixon, J., Alexander, M. D., Babo, G., & McNeese, R. (Eds.). (2014, Spring). *NCPEA Educational leadership review of doctoral research.* National Council of Professors of Educational Administration. https://www.ncpeapublications.org/ attachments/category/53/ELRDR_Spring14_Final2.pdf

Morgan, H. (2020, December). Misunderstood and mistreated: Students of color in special education. *Voices of Reform: Educational Research to Inform and Reform, 3*(2). https://files.eric.ed.gov/fulltext/ED610548.pdf

Muñiz, J. (2019, September 23). *5 ways culturally responsive teaching benefits learners.* New America. https://www.newamerica.org/education-policy/edcentral/5-ways-culturally-responsive-teaching-benefits-learners/

National Center for Education Statistics. (2019a, February). *Indicator 8: English language learners in public schools.* Institute of Education Sciences. https://nces.ed.gov/programs/raceindicators/indicator_rbc.asp

National Center for Education Statistics. (2019b, February). *Indicator 9: Students with disabilities.* Institute of Education Sciences. https://nces.ed.gov/programs/raceindicators/indicator_rbd.asp

National Center for Education Statistics. (2020). *Racial/ethnic enrollment in public schools.* https://nces.ed.gov/programs/coe/indicator_cge.asp

National Education Association. (2021–2022). *National Education Association Policy Statements.* https://www.nea.org/sites/default/files/2021-09/NEA%20Policy%20Statements%202021-2022_0.pdf

National Education Association Center for Advocacy and Outreach. (2015). *The road to student success: A toolkit for student-centered advocacy.* https://www.nea.org/sites/default/files/2020-06/The_Road_To_Student_Success%282%29.pdf

National League of Cities. (2021, July 21). What does it mean to be an anti-racist? https://www.nlc.org/article/2020/07/21/what-does-it-mean-to-be-an-anti-racist/

National PTA. (2020). *Our commitment to diversity, equity and inclusion.* https://www.pta.org/docs/default-source/default-document-library/dei-brief-final-072720.pdf

National School Climate Center. (2007). *What is school climate?* https://schoolclimate.org/about/our-approach/what-is-school-climate/

Neckerman, K. M. (2007). *Schools betrayed: Roots of failure in inner-city education.* University of Chicago Press. https://doi.org/10.7208/chicago/9780226569628.001.0001

Oakes, J. (2005). *Keeping track: How schools structure inequality* (2nd ed.). Yale University Press.

Opper, I. M. (2019a). *How teacher effectiveness spills over into other classrooms.* RAND. https://www.rand.org/pubs/research_briefs/RB10066.html

Opper, I. M. (2019b). *Teachers matter: Understanding teachers' impact on student achievement.* RAND. https://doi.org/10.7249/RR4312

Opper, I. M. (2019c). *Value-added modeling 101: Using test scores to help measure teaching effectiveness.* RAND. https://doi.org/10.7249/RR4312.1

Perry, A. M., Rothwell, J., & Harshbarger, D. (2018, November 27). *The devaluation of assets in Black neighborhoods.* Brookings. https://www.brookings.edu/research/devaluation-of-assets-in-black-neighborhoods/

Pirtle, W. (2019, April 23). The other segregation. *The Atlantic*. https://www.theatlantic.com/education/archive/2019/04/gifted-and-talented-programs-separate-students-race/587614/

Portes, P. (2005). *Dismantling educational inequality: A cultural-historical approach to closing the achievement gap*. Peter Lang.

Pumariega A. J., Jo, Y., Beck, B., & Rahmani, M. (2022, April). Trauma and U.S. minority children and youth. *Current Psychiatry Reports, 24*(4), 285–295. doi: 10.1007/s11920-022-01336-1

Rochester City School District. (2012). *Teacher evaluation guide*. https://www.nctq.org/dmsView/Rochester_Teacher_Evaluation_Guide_AUGUST_2012

Sachs, J. (2022, January 24). *Steep rise in gag orders, many sloppily drafted*. Pen America 100. https://pen.org/steep-rise-gag-orders-many-sloppily-drafted/

The Sentencing Project. (2023). *Growth in mass incarceration*. https://www.sentencingproject.org/research/

Shores, K., Kim, H. E., & Still, M. (2020, February 21). *Categorical inequalities between Black and white students are common in US schools—but they don't have to be*. Brookings. https://www.brookings.edu/blog/brown-center-chalkboard/2020/02/21/categorical-inequalities-between-black-and-white-students-are-common-in-us-schools-but-they-dont-have-to-be/

Sparks, S. D. (2019, April 30). Wealthier enclaves breaking away from school districts. *Education Week*. https://www.edweek.org/leadership/wealthier-enclaves-breaking-away-from-school-districts/2019/04

Stubbs, V. (2019). *The six pillars of a brave space*. University of Maryland. https://www.ssw.umaryland.edu/media/ssw/field-education/2---The-6-Pillars-of-Brave-Space.pdf?&

Sudderth, A. (n.d.). What is student-centered learning and why is it important? https://xqsuperschool.org/teaching-learning/what-is-student-centered-learning/

TNTP. (2018, September 25). *The opportunity myth: What students can show us about how school is letting them down—and how to fix it*. https://tntp.org/publications/view/the-opportunity-myth

Tomlinson, C. A. (2023, May). Teach up for equity and excellence. *Educational Leadership, 80*(8), 28–34. https://www.ascd.org/el/articles/teach-up-for-equity-and-excellence

Tyson, K. (2013). Tracking, segregation, and the opportunity gap: What we know and why it matters. In P. L. Carter & K. G. Welner (Eds.), *Closing the opportunity gap: What America must do to give every child an even chance* (pp. 168–180). Oxford Academic.

Tyson, K., Darity, W., Jr., & Castellino, D. R. (2005). It's not "a Black thing": Understanding the burden of acting White and other dilemmas of high achievement. *American Sociological Review, 70*(4), 582–605. https://psycnet.apa.org/doi/10.1177/000312240507000403

University of Michigan. (2023). *Practicing anti-racism and anti-racist pedagogy: An overview.* https://sites.lsa.umich.edu/inclusive-teaching/anti-racist-practices/

University of Washington Center for Educational Leadership. (2022). *Inquiry cycle: A continuous improvement tool to assist principal supervisors and principals in becoming equity-driven school leaders.* https://k-12leadership.org/tools/instructional-leadership-inquiry-cycle-tool/

U.S. Census Bureau. (2021, August 12). *2020 U.S. population more racially and ethnically diverse than measured in 2010.* https://www.census.gov/library/stories/2021/08/2020-united-states-population-more-racially-ethnically-diverse-than-2010.html

U.S. Department of Education. (n.d.). Every Student Succeeds Act (ESSA). https://www.ed.gov/essa?src=rn

U.S. Department of Education. (2021, August 9). *OSEP releases fast facts on the race and ethnicity of children with disabilities served under IDEA Part B.* https://sites.ed.gov/osers/2021/08/osep-releases-fast-facts-on-the-race-and-ethnicity-of-children-with-disabilities-served-under-idea-part-b/

U.S. Department of Education Office for Civil Rights. (2014a, March). *Data snapshot: College and career readiness* (Issue Brief No. 3). https://www2.ed.gov/about/offices/list/ocr/docs/crdc-college-and-career-readiness-snapshot.pdf

U.S. Department of Education Office for Civil Rights. (2014b, March). *Data snapshot: School discipline* (Issue Brief No. 1). https://ocrdata.ed.gov/assets/downloads/CRDC-School-Discipline-Snapshot.pdf

U.S. Department of Education Office for Civil Rights. (2014c, March). *Data snapshot: Teacher equity* (Issue Brief No. 4). https://www2.ed.gov/about/offices/list/ocr/docs/crdc-teacher-equity-snapshot.pdf

Visible Learning. (2023). *Hattie ranking: 252 influences and effect sizes related to student achievement.* https://visible-learning.org/hattie-ranking-influences-effect-sizes-learning-achievement/

Weissberg, R. (2016, February 15). Why social and emotional learning is essential for students. *Edutopia.* https://www.edutopia.org/blog/why-sel-essential-for-students-weissberg-durlak-domitrovich-gullotta

Will, M. (2017, February 6). Study: Teacher satisfaction, collaboration are keys to student achievement. *Education Week.* https://www.edweek.org/teaching-learning/study-teacher-satisfaction-collaboration-are-keys-to-student-achievement/2017/02

youth.gov. (n.d.). *Impact of family engagement.* https://youth.gov/youth-topics/impact-family-engagement

INDEX

ability grouping, 7–8
achievement. *See also* success
    culturally responsive curriculum and, 15
    teachers of color and, 9, 40
achievement gaps
    defined, 4
    factors influencing, 6–9
    fiscal effects, 3
    group-based, 6
    history of in the U.S., 4–6
    moral responsibility for eliminating, 4
    systemic and institutional racism and, 2–3
adequacy factor in achievement, 7
African American education, major eras in, 7
alumni relations, building, 35
antiracism, 10
assessment
    aligning to standards, 18
    of assets in the community, 89–90
    of equity and inclusion, 69
assignments, aligning to standards, 18
assimilation, opposition to, 8
at-risk students, meeting the needs of, 59

bias, evaluating and offsetting implicit, 19–20
BIPOC students, access to high-level and AP
    courses, vii, 17–18
Black students
    with Black teachers, achievement and, 9, 40
    disciplinary removals and dropouts, vii
    effective teachers, likelihood of having,
        26–27
    percent receiving special education services,
        vii
brave spaces, 29–31, 41–43
budget and finance team, central office, 61–62

capital project planning, 62
celebrations, role of, 64, 75

central office teams
    qualities of antiracist, 50–51
    roadblocks faced by, 62–63
    strategies to accelerate progress toward anti-
        racist goals, 63–64
central office teams, landmarks of antiracist
    budget and finance, 61–62
    communications, 57–58
    community engagement, 55–57
    data and accountability, 52–54
    human resources, 60–61
    student support, 58–60
    teaching and learning, 54–55
central office teams, roles of antiracist
    address student trauma, 60
    at-risk students, meet the needs of, 59
    bond referendums for capital project plan-
        ning, 62
    community partners, identify, 55–56
    culturally responsive curriculum, support for
        implementation, 54
    data disaggregation, 52
    discipline practices, develop nondiscrimi-
        natory, 60
    district goals, develop and monitor, 52–53
    family engagement, 53, 56
    inclusive and equitable goals, identify, 53
    interrogate factors contributing to racial
        inequities, 53–54
    leverage funds for strategic support, 61–62
    multitiered system of supports (MTSS), 58–59
    pipeline programs, 61
    place highly qualified staff at schools with
        greatest needs, 61
    professional development, 54–55
    systems and resources supports, 55–57
    tell the story of equity work, 57–58
    training programs, 61
    user-friendly messaging, 57

challenges, addressing by district leaders, 75
Civil Rights Act, 6
classroom audits, 22
classroom observations, 27, 40
classrooms, antiracist
        brave spaces in, 29–30, 41–43
        roadblocks to establishing, 31–34
climate, school, 39
college enrollment, Black students, 9
communication
        conversation norms and guidelines, 42
        start the conversation for partnerships, 90
        user-friendly messaging, 57
communications team, central office, 57–58
community, landmarks of the antiracist
        community equity committees, 85–88
        elected officials, support from, 84–85
        equity-centered community partners, 83–84
        family empowerment, 80–82
        student advocacy and agency supports, 79–80
community, roles for the antiracist
        district leaders, engaging with, 86
        family engagement, 81–82
        financial investments, 84
        increase representation across ethnicity,
            race, and religion, 83
        leadership skills, building family and student,
            80, 82
        opportunity gaps, address, 84
        social capital, build students', 83–84
        students as co-creators of solutions, engag-
            ing, 79–80
community, the antiracist
        importance of, 77–78
        power of, 77–78
        roadblocks for the, 88–89
        shortcuts for the, 89–90
community, valuing, 40
community engagement, case study, 100
community engagement team, central office,
    55–57
community equity committees, 85–88
community partnerships
        central office team for, 55–56
        district leaders, shortcuts for, 75
        educational equity, case studies, 105
conversation norms and guidelines, 42
core values, identified and embedded by leader-
    ship, 68
courage, quality of, 73–74
critical race theory (CRT), 73–74
critical thinking in brave spaces, 30
cultural competence, 15–17, 70–71
culture, defined, 39
curriculum, antiracist
        central office team role in, 54
        defined, 14
        functions and benefits of, 14–15
        legislating, 21

curriculum, antiracist (continued)
        roadblocks to implementing, 21–22
        students of color reflected in the, 13–14
curriculum, implementing an antiracist
        address areas lacking diverse representation,
            20
        assignments and assessments aligned to
            standards, 18
        BIPOC content. continuous inclusion of, 23
        classroom audits in, 22
        enrichment and learning extensions pro-
            vided, 19
        materials audits, 19–20
        researching for, 16
        students with learning gaps, engaging, 18–19
        student voice and choice in, 23
        thinking skills, pushing higher-order, 18
        understand the lived experience, 16–17
curriculum, landmarks of an antiracist
        bias, intentional probing for, 19–20
        cultural responsiveness, 15–17
        inclusivity, 15–17
        rigor, focus on, 17–19
curriculum and instruction team, central office,
    54–55
curriculum resources improvement, case study,
    100

data, interrogate racialized through an equity
    lens, 44–45
data and accountability team, central office, 52–54
data disaggregation, 52
discipline policies and practices
        case study, 104–105
        central office team role in, 60
        racial inequity in, 2–3
district goals, develop and monitor, 52–53
district leaders, antiracist
        importance of, 66
        roadblocks faced by, 73–74
        shortcuts for, 75, 86
district leaders, landmarks of antiracist
        expectations, clear and high, 70–71
        vision for equity, 67–69
        whole educator approach, 71–72
district leaders, qualities of antiracist
        core values, identified and embedded, 68
        courage, 73–74
        cultural competence and perspectives
            valued, 70–71
        equity and inclusion assessments, 69
        expectations linked to policies, 68–69
        leadership pipeline, building an effective, 70
        legislative relationships, 74
        overview, 66–67
        recruitment, hiring, and retention, 71, 74
        self-care, 73
        staff, respecting and responding to, 72
        teacher efficacy, increasing collective, 72

early adopters, engaging, 104
education
    African American, major eras in, 7
    whole child approach to, 28–29
educational equity, case studies
    Acorn School District, 99–101
    Beacon School System, 101–103
    Cleverton Public Schools, 103–105
    community backlash to equity work, addressing, 101–103
    community partnerships, 105
    a community rallying cry, 99–101
    curriculum resources, improvement in, 100
    disciplinary practices, improving, 104–105
    early adopters, engaging, 104
    equity policy development, 101
    professional development, 100–101
    relationship building, school board, 102
    student enrichment, increasing access to, 101, 105
    successes and perspectives shared, 102–103
    teacher capacity, building, 103–105
educational equity, defined, xi, 1
educational inequity. *See* achievement gaps
education debt, 7
elected officials, community involvement, 84–85
Elementary and Secondary Education Act, 5–6
emotional well-being, supporting student, 60
engagement, rigor and, 18–19
enrichment, 19
Equality of Educational Opportunity (Coleman report), 6
equity
    assessment, 69
    factor influencing achievement, 6
    roadblocks to, 46, 73–74, 88–89
equity-centered community partners, 83–84
equity policy development, case study, 101
equity work, opposition to, 88–89
Every Student Succeeds Act (ESSA), 5–6
expectations
    culturally responsive curriculum, 15
    high, maintaining, 27–28
    high and clear, expressed by district leaders, 70–71
    linked to policies by district leaders, 68–69
    low, calling-in, 32

families
    empowering by the community, 80–82
    engagement by central office teams, 53, 56
fear, leaning into, 30
fear of change roadblock, 73
financial investments by the community, 84
funding for strategic support, central office teams, 61–62

Great Resignation, 74–75

human resources team, central office, 60–61

incarceration rates, schools contribution to, 3
inclusion assessments, 69
inclusivity
    community misunderstandings as roadblock, 73–74
    curricular, 15–17
intentions, examining in brave spaces, 30

leadership pipeline, building an effective, 70, 96–97
leadership shortcut for antiracist teachers, 35
leadership skills, building family, 82
learning extension, 19
legislative relationships, 74

messaging, user-friendly, 57
mindfulness in brave spaces, 30–31
mindsets, fixed, 46–47
multitiered system of supports (MTSS), 58–59

No Child Left Behind (NCLB) Act, 5–6
nonracism, 10

onboarding programs, 71
opportunity gaps, community addressing, 84
oppositional culture theory, 8

pedagogy, culturally responsive, 14–17
perspectives
    honoring others,' 30
    sharing, case study, 102–103
police brutality, 3
policing in schools, 2–3
power sharing, resistance as roadblock, 88
professional development, 54–55, 100–101

racism, systemic in education, 2–4
real estate industry, redlining in the, 2
receivement gap, 7
reciprocity and achievement, 7
redlining, 2
relationship building
    central office teams, 63–64
    community partnerships, 75
    school board, case studies, 102
    as shortcut for teachers and leaders, 34–35, 40, 48
resources
    case study, 100
    central office teams role in, 55–57
    deficits as roadblock, 47

safe spaces, 29
scaffolding, 18–19
school leaders
    roadblocks faced by antiracist, 46–47
    school success and effectiveness of, 38
    shortcuts for antiracist, 48

school leaders, landmarks of antiracist
  brave spaces supported, 41–42
  intervention and enrichment provisions, 43–44
  racialized data, interrogate through an equity lens, 44–45
  school culture and climate, building a positive, 39–40
school leaders, qualities of antiracist
  community and diversity valued, 40
  conversation norms and guidelines established, 42
  overview, 38–39
  select and value antiracist teacher and staff, 40
  staff and student voice amplified, 41–42
schools
  capital project planning, 62
  creating equity-focused, requirements for, 25
  culture and climate, building a positive, 39–40
  funding, racial inequity in, 2
  policing in, 2–3
school segregation, 2
school-to-prison pipeline, 3
self-care, 73
skills, lack of as roadblock, 63
social-emotional learning (SEL), 28–29
staff
  celebrating, 75
  effect of racial congruence for, 8–9
  highly qualified, placing at schools with greatest needs, 61
  respecting and responding to needs of, 72
  voice, amplifying, 41–42
standards
  aligning assignments and assessments to, 18
  teaching for culturally responsive, 21–22
story of equity work, central office for telling the, 57–58
structural racism, 2
student advocacy groups, 35–36
student enrichment and learning extensions
  increasing access to, 19, 101, 105
  school leaders, landmark of, 43–44
students. See also Black students
  at-risk, meeting the needs of, 59
  BIPOC, access to high-level and AP courses, vii, 17–18
  as co-creators of equity solutions, 79–80
  leadership skills, building, 80
  social capital, building, 83–84
  voice and choice, increasing, 23, 41–42
student support team, central office, 58–60
student trauma, addressing, 60
success. See also achievement
  academic, key ingredients required for, 17
  of district leaders, requirements for, 66–67

success (continued)
  school, leadership and, 38
  sharing as shortcut, 75
  sharing case study, 102–103
superintendents. See entries for district leaders
systemic change, steps in leading
  action plans, 92–93
  celebrate wins, 95–96
  course corrections, 95
  equity audits, 92
  focus on equity, 94
  goals identification, 92–93
  implementation, 93–94
  progress monitoring, 94
  solutions, identifying technical and adaptive, 93
  wellness and self-care, 95–96
systemic change, sustaining
  collaboration and transparency, 96
  communication and feedback, 96
  internal and external capacity building, 96–97
  parting advice, 97

teacher efficacy, increasing collective, 72
teacher quality, defined, 9
teachers
  early adopters, engaging, 104
  qualities of antiracist, 25–26
  racial congruence, effect of, 8–9
  recruitment, hiring, and retention, 40, 61, 71, 74
  roadblocks for antiracist, 32–34
  strategies overcoming roadblocks, 34–36
  talent development, 61, 96
  warm demanders, 27–28
teachers, landmarks of antiracist
  brave spaces environments, 29–31
  effectiveness, 26–27
  high expectations, 27–28
  whole child approach, 28–29
teacher salaries, 26, 27
teacher shortages, 26, 74, 96
teachers of color, achievement and, 8–9, 40
teaching quality, 9, 19
thinking skills, requiring higher-order, 18
tracking, 7–8, 17
training, 61, 63–64

value-added model of effectiveness, 27
values, identifying and embedding by leadership, 68
vision for equity, 67–69
vulnerability, defined, 30

warm demanders, 27–28
wellness spaces, 48
whole child approach, 28–29
whole educator approach, 71–72

ABOUT THE AUTHORS

Avis Williams, EdD, is the superintendent of NOLA Public Schools, the first woman to serve permanently in the role. She leads through equity, excellence and joy, and her core values. A native of Salisbury, North Carolina, she has served in leadership positions in the U.S. Army, as an entrepreneur, and a school administrator. She received an undergraduate degree from Athens State University, master's degrees from Alabama A&M and Jacksonville State Universities, and an education specialist degree and a doctorate from the University of Alabama.

Avis has been an elementary, middle, and high school principal. She was executive director of curriculum and instruction in North Carolina, where she led instruction for more than 60 schools, and an assistant superintendent in Tuscaloosa City (Alabama) Schools. Prior to her historic appointment to lead NOLA Public Schools, she served as superintendent of Selma City (Alabama) Schools for five years.

An award-winning leader and sought-after speaker, Avis grew up in poverty and is passionate about improving outcomes for all children in the community she serves. A finalist for Alabama Superintendent of the Year, she was named a National School Public Relations Association Superintendent to Watch and received the University of Alabama's Dr. Harold Bishop Leadership Award and the AASA Dr. Effie Jones Humanitarian Award.

Avis's joy comes from spending time with her daughter, Briahna, and from running, writing, and being a "dog mom" to her standard poodles, Coco and Butterscotch. She also enjoys giving back to her community. A past president of the ASCD Board of Directors, Avis has served on the boards of numerous nonprofit organizations and is a member of Rotary International, the Links, Inc., and Delta Sigma Theta, Inc.

 **Brenda Elliott, EdD,** is chief of equity in DC Public Schools. As the first person hired in this role, she led the development of the district's equity framework and oversaw the launch of Adelante, the district's first Latino/Latinx Leadership Summit, and the establishment of Anti-Racist Educator University (ARE-U). She serves as an adjunct professor in American University's Antiracist Administration, Supervision, and Leadership (ARASL) graduate certificate program and is helping to support our next generation of antiracist educational leaders.

Bren has 30 years of experience as a public school educator working to address racialized gaps in student outcomes. She works nationally to build and connect with equity leaders and to support women and people of color. As an officer in the U.S. Army, she served as the Equal Opportunity Officer for her battalion. She is a graduate of DC's Seeding Disruptions' Equity Fellowship and Leading4Equity's Women's Superintendent Policy Leadership Program. Bren was an inaugural member of AASA's Equity Cohort, which published a case study based on the tremendous equity work she led in DC.

Bren's awards include National Alliance of Black School Educators' Principal of the Year and the AASA Dr. Effie Jones Humanitarian Award. She was awarded High Point University's Surratt Outstanding Doctoral Student Award for her dissertation, "District-Level Equity Leaders' Approaches to Addressing the Racial Achievement Gap Between Black and White Students in Urban Public Schools," which addressed a gap in research regarding the role, experiences, and impact of equity leaders in school districts.

In addition to being an equity warrior, Bren loves spending time with her beautiful and brilliant grandchildren, gardening, engaging with Delta Sigma Theta Sorority, Inc., and all things "beach."

Related ASCD Resources: Equity and Equity Leadership

At the time of publication, the following resources were available (ASCD stock numbers in parentheses).

Building Equity: Policies and Practices to Empower All Learners by Dominique Smith, Nancy Frey, Ian Pumpian, and Douglas Fisher (#117031)

Cultural Competence Now: 56 Exercises to Help Educators Understand and Challenge Bias, Racism, and Privilege by Vernita Mayfield (#118043)

Culture, Class, and Race: Constructive Conversations That Unite and Energize Your School and Community by Brenda CampbellJones, Shannon Keeny, and Franklin CampbellJones (#118010)

The Equity & Social Justice Education 50: Critical Questions for Improving Opportunities and Outcomes for Black Students by Baruti K. Kafele (#121060)

Five Practices for Equity-Focused School Leadership by Sharon I. Radd, Gretchen Givens Generett, Mark Anthony Gooden, and George Theoharis (#120008)

Leading Within Systems of Inequity in Education: A Liberation Guide for Leaders of Color by Mary Rice-Boothe (#123014)

Leading Your School Toward Equity: A Practical Framework for Walking the Talk by Dwayne Chism (#123003)

Stay and Prevail: Students of Color Don't Need to Leave Their Communities to Succeed by Nancy Gutiérrez and Roberto Padilla (#123006)

Support and Retain Educators of Color: 6 Principles for Culturally Affirming Leadership by Andrea Terrero Gabbadon (#123018)

For up-to-date information about ASCD resources, go to. You can search the complete archives of *Educational Leadership* at www.ascd.org/el. To contact us, send an email to member@ascd.org or call 1-800-933-2723 or 703-578-9600.

ascd whole child

The ASCD Whole Child approach is an effort to transition from a focus on narrowly defined academic achievement to one that promotes the long-term development and success of all children. Through this approach, ASCD supports educators, families, community members, and policymakers as they move from a vision about educating the whole child to sustainable, collaborative actions.

The Antiracist Roadmap to Educational Equity relates to all five tenets. For more about the ASCD Whole Child approach, visit **www.ascd.org/wholechild.**

WHOLE CHILD
TENETS

1 HEALTHY
Each student enters school healthy and learns about and practices a healthy lifestyle.

2 SAFE
Each student learns in an environment that is physically and emotionally safe for students and adults.

3 ENGAGED
Each student is actively engaged in learning and is connected to the school and broader community.

4 SUPPORTED
Each student has access to personalized learning and is supported by qualified, caring adults.

5 CHALLENGED
Each student is challenged academically and prepared for success in college or further study and for employment and participation in a global environment.